T0373320

peter opsvik

rethinking sitting

W. W. Norton & Company
New York & London

Copyright (c) 2008 by Gaidaros Forlag AS, Oslo
First American Edition 2009

All rights reserved
Printed in Singapore

For information about permission to reproduce selections from this book, write to
Permissions, W. W. Norton & Company, Inc., 500 Fifth Avenue, New York, NY 10110

For information about special discounts for bulk
purchases, please contact W. W. Norton
Special Sales at specialsales@wwnorton.com or 800-233-4830

Cover design: W. W. Norton & Company, Inc.,
Graphic design, typesetting and layout: Peter Knudsen, GRAF as, Norway
Set with FF DIN 9,5/11 pt

Manufacturing by KHL
Production manager: Leeann Graham

Library of Congress Cataloging-in-Publication Data

Opsvik, Peter, 1939–
Rethinking sitting / Peter Opsvik. -- 1st American ed.
     p. cm.
Includes index.
ISBN 978-0-393-73288-7 (pbk.)
1. Chair design. 2. Sitting position. I. Title.
NK2715.O67 2008
749'.32--dc22

                              2008049969

ISBN: 978-0-393-73288-7 (pbk.)

W. W. Norton & Company, Inc., 500 Fifth Avenue, New York, N.Y. 10110
www.wwnorton.com
W. W. Norton & Company Ltd., Castle House, 75/76 Wells Street, London W1T 3QT

0 9 8 7 6 5 4 3 2 1

Almost all European cities have pedestrian areas or malls where various entertainers do their best to attract people's attention. It has often struck me that the largest crowds almost invariably gather around these characters who stand still – impersonating statues. The feat of remaining completely still and not doing anything thus arouses more interest than the antics of acrobats and jugglers. This tells us that moving is part of our natural behaviour and that Man in a still or static state strikes us as artificial – so artificial that we are willing to pay to watch the spectacle.

rethinking sitting

For millions of years on Earth the human race has led physically active lives. Throughout the last two centuries, industrialization resulted in physical inactivity and increased use of the sitting position for more and more people. In a growing number of societies, chairs and furniture for sitting have become standard pieces of equipment in the workplace, in institutions and in private homes. With few exceptions these sitting devices were designed according to the established standards for chairs, based on the accepted "western" way of sitting.

In this book I address the question of whether or not this is the only, most functional design for the human body whenever we assume the sitting posture. The solutions that are presented in this book are primarily intended for users who remain sedentary for extended periods of time and for use in those parts of the world where people's physical condition and work tasks have made them dependent on such means of support. I specify this because it is not my belief that everyone needs sitting devices, nor that all sitting devices need such functionality.

Industrial design has, of course, a set of quality criteria, such as visual form, ease of production, transportability, technical quality, durability, ecology, use of materials, use of resources, recycling, etc. Although functional content – particularly relating to ergonomic criteria – is the main subject of this book, this does not mean that the other criteria are of less importance, but simply that they are not my focus here. However, it is difficult to be entirely consistent, so other design criteria such as, for example, environment and flexibility will also be touched upon.

Chapter 1 Why – Backdrop is theoretical and contains articles that illustrate people's physical life throughout history in general, as well as their relationship to the sitting posture in particular.

Chapter 2 How – Theory presents underlying principles for various theoretical solutions.

Chapter 3 Favourite Postures
In this section, I intend to look at the postures that various parts of our anatomy prefer when we are sitting and what support devices they are most comfortable with.

Chapters 4 Tilting, 5 Support, and 6 Size
The theories from previous chapters materialize or evolve into physical solutions, all of which have one thing in common: they give priority to the needs of the human body while sitting.

Chapter 7 Other Qualities than the Ergonomic
Perhaps we could call the examples in chapters 4, 5 and 6 "creations for motion", and the examples in chapter 7 "creations for emotion"? More precisely stated, this chapter presents examples of products or objects where qualities other than the ergonomic are paramount.

Chapter 8 Observations and Inspirations
Although ergonomics is the main topic of this book, in this chapter I examine some other aspects of my field.

This book is not intended to be read from cover to cover, but is rather envisaged more as a reference work. For the book to function in this manner, some of the same points will be repeated. For example, the product explanations may reiterate topics covered in the theoretical part, and for this I ask for the reader's understanding. To keep repetitions to a minimum, I also refer readers to other articles they may read to obtain a complete understanding of a product.

I hope this book will contain useful information for everyone who, for professional, educational or personal reasons, is interested in sitting solutions – as all of us who live in a sedentary society should be.

With a few exceptions,
my solutions for furniture
products can be divided into
two broad categories situated
at opposite ends of a scale:

← Rational and
ergonomic at
the one end

Emotional and
expressionist at
the other end →

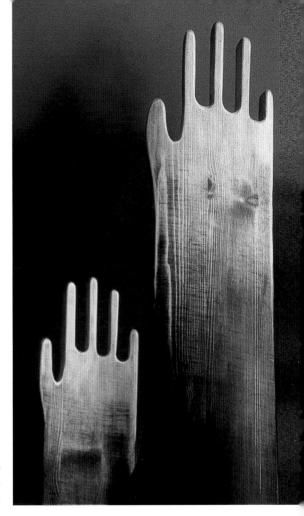

chapter 1
why – backdrop

Our active past

How has the human race fared so far?
In the Stone Age and in nomadic societies, people led physically active lives.

Constant walking, hunting and picking things up off the ground and down from trees were prerequisites for finding food. Even after people began to settle into agricultural societies with permanent abodes, the physical labour necessary for survival depended upon a varied use of the body – of the head, trunk and limbs and of the muscles and joints.

Over thousands of years, our bodies have tried to satisfy our needs by providing us with strength, speed, suppleness, flexibility and mobility. This is simply the kind of lifestyle that our bodies are designed for.

In addition, each of us has our own personal active past – in the form of our childhood – which for most people of my generation was filled with physical activity from dawn till dusk, playing outside in the woods, fields and streets.

Nomadic people regarded all forms of sitting or immobility as harmful, while people who settled in villages regarded sitting as sacred (Hajo Eickhoff).

Our passive present

Recently, however, across large parts of the globe, lifestyles have changed radically and have become much more sedate. There is less variety in the kinds of physical tasks we expect our bodies to perform. For some groups of people, this change started some 5 000 years ago; for others, the change came a mere 50 years ago. Although we can regard these changes as a long process in historical terms, 5 000 years is in fact just a tiny fraction of human history. An all-pervasive change in the way we live has thus occurred in what amounts to a blink of the eye, when viewed from the perspective of the evolutionary history of the human body.

Many children, for example, experienced a sudden change in lifestyle. From being participants throughout their youth in the active and varied life of their adult role models, the young now belong to societies which have obligatory schooling.

Being required to sit at a school desk for large portions of the day represented a great change in itself, and the situation was not made better by the fact that the ideal pupil in most societies was the one who sat as still as possible! At the beginning of the 1800s, the school system in Prussia was based on a military model. Classes were called in for compulsory schooling. The expression "Prussian discipline" reveals the adult view of restless pupils during that era.

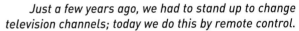

Just a few years ago, we had to stand up to change television channels; today we do this by remote control.

Post-industrialized societies

Physical mobility began to decrease with the advent of industrialized and subsequently post-industrialized societies. We move less and less, as our work is often stationary and involves repeating the same movement again and again, for hours on end, day after day. We have abandoned varied use of our bodies, and for most of us, hard physical exertion is no longer essential to our survival. On the contrary, we invest both money and creativity in eliminating reasons for normal and positive use of the body. Doors open automatically, escalators replace stairs, moving walkways reduce the number of steps we have to take at the airport, ski lifts pull us up to the top of the slalom slope, drive-in fast food outlets mean we can get dinner without getting out of the car – we even have electric toothbrushes to prevent our arms from getting tired in the name of dental hygiene.

Staring at a screen for hours on end is a relatively new activity that is spreading like wildfire. First there was the television screen, then the computer screen, and now we are seeing the advent of mini-ature portable screens in the form of palmtops and mobile phones everywhere. Our eyes are designed to alternate between looking down and scrutinizing something we have in our hands and looking up at far-off objects in the natural surroundings. Spending large portions of our day staring at a screen that is a fixed distance from us entails a lack of variation not only for our eyes but also for our posture. If you include all the screens you look at, from the TV at home, in the café, on the train or wherever, to the PC at work, etc., this can easily add up to more than 50% of our day being spent in front of a screen.

Just a few decades ago, most children walked or rode bicycles to school and spent much of their free time playing outdoors in the garden or in the street. Nowadays, it is not uncommon for children to start the day with cartoons on television at breakfast time. Soon they will be able to watch films on the school bus, too. Teaching is increasingly screen-based, and children also spend a lot of their free time watching TV and playing computer games. All these changes mean children are less mobile than they used to be and their bodies are deprived of natural, innate and healthy activities.

Scientific papers and other research highlight the unhealthy way most of us are living, and results show that we are less active than we used to be. The gap between people who are physically active and those who are not is widening. An increasing proportion of the population is now much less active than was the case just a few decades ago. Military recruits are in worse physical condition than they once were, and the average weight of forty-year-olds has increased dramatically, despite a lower calorie intake.

Tools

Homo habilis is over two million years old, and yet the idea of attaching a handle to a stone occurred only 30 000 years ago. How many hundred thousands of years of hammering with a hand-held stone had to pass before someone came up with the idea of the axe? It took an awfully long time – as well as a huge product development team – to develop the "product". Compare this to the extremely rapid development of tools we have experienced in the rich parts of the world over recent centuries.

What is the cause of this new lack of mobility and variety? Should we blame our tools?

When Homo habilis started using tools, this marked the beginning of a new era fostering a new lifestyle, which unfortunately for many of us has led to monotony and passivity.

Most tools or equipment are intended to make our lives easier, more efficient and more comfortable. The stone axe made it easier to cut trees, the plough simplified farming, the bow and arrow made hunting more efficient, and so on. We should, of course, be grateful for all the strenuous labour that our tools have eliminated and for the improved standard of living they provide us. As a designer, I feel it is important to examine both the negative and positive effects that tools have on our lives. We need to be aware of all of the possible consequences that tools may cause for our bodies and the way we live.

The negative aspects of exaggerated and monotonous use of tools can be grouped into two major categories: load and repetition. The 100 female skeletons dating back 10 000 years that were found some time ago in Northern Syria had deformed toes, backs and knee joints. The women suffered from occupational musculoskeletal disorders as a result of poor posture and the repetition of movements.

For society, the invention of a device to grind corn was a major leap forwards, but for the individuals who performed this monotonous work, using the tool as part of a specialized division of labour, this contraption entailed a serious deterioration in their quality of life.

Excessive physical labour
It is probably safe to assume that in "pre-tool" societies, hard physical labour seven days a week was the main cause of many aches and pains. Or perhaps most work-related injuries in former times were caused by accidents.

Monotony
The widespread use of tools, machines and motorized forms of transport entailed fewer opportunities for varied use of the body, and greater monotony. This in its turn became the main agent of muscular and skeletal damage especially for people who use the same tools again and again over long periods of time.

Passivity
Nowadays this trend poses the main challenge in connection with occupational musculoskeletal disorders. Small muscles are used excessively and suffer overload, while the bigger muscles are hardly used at all. Active muscle work has been replaced by static work, and our bodies tolerate static use very badly, and they protest with pain. The stage is set for this to continue: more and more of us will do less and less physical labour, and our physical activities in general will be too few to keep our bodies in optimal working order.

The transition to extensive use of tools does not always lead to a better existence for the human body. It is probably better for our health to walk than to drive a car. It may be more natural for the human body to deliver a message in person than to use the various forms of transmission that began with a chisel and rock, continued via brushes, quills, pens and pencils and has culminated in the typewriter and computer, palmtops and SMS text messages. Time and again we have seen that the latest and most efficient solutions become a bane if we use them for hours and hours every day.

Whether we use two stones to grind corn, or we "grind" using the computer mouse, it amounts to the same thing. The only difference is that different parts of our body are affected.

The trend brought about by the car industry is another interesting example. In the first place, the car renders obsolete the activities we would have used to get from A to B, such as walking or riding a bike. But the ways in which we are made passive don't stop there. When we drive a car, some of the operations we perform are dynamic and are good for us, while others are static and cause problems. Depressing the clutch stretches out our left leg, we move our ankle, thereby improving blood circulation. Changing gear involves using our arm muscles, another positive aspect. We also used to get some variation from opening the window or the sunroof manually. But what did the car designers come up with? Exactly – they automated gearshifts, and clutching became unnecessary, and they introduced electric windows, making the driver as physically passive as possible.

Still, it is a high price we ultimately end up paying for removing the few arm-and-foot movements that were necessary to move mankind on four wheels. When we get home after a long drive, we have to spend our spare time "clutching and gearing" in the gym.

Nowadays, the frequency of muscle and joint injuries is increasing almost proportionally with the number of tools we use, begging the question as to whether Man is physically better equipped for life with tools, or without them?

Human life without the development of tools would entail the elimination of a key human characteristic: creativity. Creativity leads to new solutions that no one has seen before. We have an innate desire to improve things, as well as a fascination with the potential uses of completely new tools.

Of course I am aware that the general tendencies I have described above mostly apply to the so-called developed part of the world. Heavy and strenuous physical labour is a major problem for people in many professions, and the development of better tools that can alleviate their physical workload is still a very important task.

Sitting devices primarily intended for applications where users are seated over longer periods must be characterized as tools, and it is important to develop these in a way that minimizes the negative impact the tool may have on the user.

As designers, we must not focus one-sidedly on what these tools can do *for* us and forget to find out what they can do *to* us. Tools should serve the individual, the community and the environment – in both the short and long run.

In order to reintroduce meaningful physical activity in the workplace, we could try installing pedals and a dynamo under the desk, requiring the user to pedal in order to generate the electric power necessary to run the PC.

Sitting postures

In most ancient societies, sitting took up a very small part of an otherwise physically active existence. Throughout history, sitting postures, or the way we have placed our limbs while sitting, have varied from period to period, culture to culture, and continent to continent. Studies of the history of sitting have observed a connection between preferred different sitting postures and a number of social factors that affected the choice of these. Circumstances that affect sitting include the nature of one's work, climate, religion, hierarchy and perceptions of different social roles and functions.

In fact, our Western way of sitting is still far from being the norm. In some places, a cross-legged sitting posture is the most common; in others kneeling is preferred, and in yet others squatting is considered the most natural and comfortable.

Nomadic tribes, past and present, are obviously unable to cart a lot of furniture around with them, so the various postures that we refer to as sitting tended to take place on the ground or on the various formations that nature has to offer.

When the Stone Age man wanted to rest, he lay down wherever he could.

Pictures of Buddha provide perhaps the most famous images of a person sitting without any form of assistance.

Squatting, which is still widespread in Africa as well as in South Asia, may be seen as related to the human fight-or-flight reflex. It is an alert posture from which one can get on the move very quickly. This posture might have been the decisive factor in the event of an attack by an enemy or wild animal.

The formal Japanese kneeling posture, seiza, is a highly attentive posture and reflects Japanese norms of politeness.

There are also gender differences in sitting: men tend to open up and spread out more while sitting, whereas women tend to keep their limbs closer to the body midline – although it is difficult to say whether this is innate or culturally defined as well-bred femininity.

Logically, there ought to be an even greater variety of sitting postures as a result of support devices such as the chair.

We know that the human body can command an enormous repertoire of sitting postures. So why did standardization committees around the world choose a single sitting posture as the starting point for their standards? This question is highly relevant, because sitting has become such a dominant part of our everyday lives.

The ISO standard, CEN, US and S – all defined the perfect sitting posture as a right-angled, upright posture.

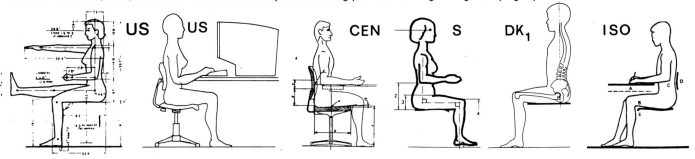

"Homo sapiens" has become "Homo sedens"

Sitting: term describing a number of postures between standing up and lying down.

If we consider for a moment what we do during the course of a day, we will discover that many of us spend a surprising amount of time in some kind of chair. An alarming number of people spend ¾ of their entire day from dawn to dusk sitting.

Our industrialized part of the world has turned into a society of sitting human beings. "Homo sapiens" has become "Homo sedens".

Information technology has introduced some additional challenges to our life of sitting: the keyboard, mouse and screen demand active fingers, eyes and brain with the rest of the body in stand-by mode. This not only entails that we spend even more time sitting, but that our sitting has become even more static.

The human race has spent 99.99% of its time on this planet as active individuals. Why is it that we suddenly find ourselves stuck in some kind of seat all day long?

We sit down to eat breakfast, we sit while travelling, we sit as we work, we sit during our breaks, we sit down to eat dinner and then we spend a lot of our free time sitting in front of the TV.

Sitting on a seat – the message of language

In many languages, the verb "to sit" also signifies holding a position of power. Idioms such as "sit on a committee" and "sit in Parliament" say more about power than about sitting. Expressions such as a "seat of learning", "the sitting bishop" and "a sitting of the court", as well as "chairman", "parliamentary seats", "to be in the chair", "to take the chair", "to chair a meeting" and the "chair" all refer to social status and powerful positions.

These examples suggest that sitting postures and sitting traditions relate as much to social circumstances as to needs for physical support.

The chair and the authority

The first formal sitting device may have been a stone or a tree stump where the leader of the tribe could sit on a higher level than the others when giving his instructions, the extra height lending him the authority he needed. Indeed, we might even ask whether status and authority were the primary functional requirements for the very first furniture designed for the seated position?

It has been widely accepted that the oldest chairs with a back and armrests date back to the age of the Pharaohs in ancient Egypt. Here is one theory as to why: in Europe it was generally easy to find a suitable object or mound in the terrain on which the leader could sit in a higher position than his subordinates, but in the desert this was more problematic. It was not easy to make a suitable platform out of sand, and so the Egyptians "invented" the chair.

Seductive as this theory is, it has since been discovered that the Egyptians were not the first people to sit on chairs. Archaeological finds in south-eastern Europe dating back some 5 700 years include depictions of people sitting on devices that can be called chairs. Another intriguing aspect of these findings is that they only show women sitting on chairs.

Historical depictions of various forms of leadership or hierarchies tend to show the "leader" figure placed higher up and in a larger chair than people of lower rank.

An important person was given his seat on a stage or podium, probably to ensure that his or her head was held higher than the heads of his subjects.

It is not difficult to understand that sitting on a carved object such as a bench, chest or stool lent the sitter more prestige than sitting on the ground or the floor. When chairs later on became a symbol of power, the back of the chair also played an important role, providing an impressive background and frame around the sitter.

If the sole purpose of sitting devices for figures of authority was to ensure leaders greater comfort, thrones would probably look quite different. Archaeological finds suggest that the ancient Pharaohs did not lean back against the vertical back of the chair. By sitting in a highly disciplined, upright fashion, the leader distanced himself from the more natural postures assumed by the lower classes. In Egypt, people also believed that an upright sitting posture enhanced contact with the higher powers.

In ancient Greece, the heavy throne or seat of honour seems to derive from Egyptian or Western Asiatic prototypes, but the Greeks took them to new heights

of grandeur and elaboration in the thrones they built for cult statues. As in Egypt, Greek chairs eventually began to assume freer, more practical forms, as is illustrated by the klismos, with its curved back and legs. The Romans went a step further in prioritizing freedom and comfort by adopting the lying position at the table.

However, despite these trends, the vertically backed chair continued to act as a symbol of official power, and this type of tall chair was still used as the symbol of power for both religious and secular leaders in Europe during the Middle Ages. Mediaeval churches can provide us with a lot of information about sitting, and I will be returning to this later.

From the Renaissance on, chairs of different types became more and more common, but they still remained the prerogative of the ruling classes. Renaissance chairs were status symbols and often resembled miniature thrones.

In recent history, the use of chairs has increased in most parts of the world. The rapidity with which this has happened and how widespread the use of chairs is varies from area to area and culture to culture, but as a general rule, one of the most important functions of chairs right up until the modern age has been to denote authority.

In the United States the term "executive chair" is currently used for an expensive work chair, but if you research the matter further to find out what is so "executive" about this chair, you will find that it is only the size. It would appear that the most important thing is for executives to have a higher seat back than their junior employees.

The Director's chair is a well-known feature on film sets. It is not exactly magnificent, but the observant watcher will notice that there are not many other people on the set who have their own chairs. And should the Director's chair become available, very few members of the crew would even consider sitting in it.

The industrial revolution and social mobility

The eighteenth century, with its rapid turnover of styles, also brought with it a more widespread use of chairs. Chairs were no longer the sole privilege of the aristocracy, but they were still more or less the privilege of the well-to-do.

Around 1830, the craftsman Thonet started making chairs by bending pre-steamed wood. These chairs became the forerunners of the bentwood furniture that conquered a huge portion of the European and American mass market during the second half of the century. Mass produced furniture was coming into its own, and chairs became a regular feature of every-day life for large segments of society in the industrialized world.

In the nineteenth century, the major changes brought about by industrialization led to chairs becoming a standard piece of equipment in the workplace, schools and private homes. However, it was not only the new means of production that caused the general spread of chairs. Industrialization also led to more and more people performing their work whilst sitting. It is clear that the factory worker's and the office worker's work chairs were designed according to the established chair standard, based on the accepted way of sitting in the upper echelons of society. No analyses were performed to determine which postures and ergonomic solutions were best suited to the work in question.

There were actually professions in the industrialized world, which for a long time resisted this rigid tendency and kept their particular work postures: tailors continued to sit in the tailor position, book keepers stood at high desks, cobblestone layers had their mushroom-shaped stools. However, these were the exceptions to the rule. In general, "elegant" body language and rules of etiquette emulated in the desire for upward social mobility may have been as decisive a factor in determining "sitting codes" as the shape of the chairs themselves.

The similarity between the Pharaoh's throne and the clerk's chair shows us how we took after upper class culture rather than trying to find good working postures when the modern chair was constructed. We kept on trying to emulate the Pharaohs, the mediaeval kings and the renaissance bourgeoisie.

Even in countries with very different ideals regarding what is the proper way to sit, the all-pervasiveness of Western culture has begun to prevail over local traditions. For example, in Japan, Western furnishings are taking over at the expense of rooms where normally the only sitting device is the tatami mat.

We noticed in the 1980s that when people in high positions choose our alternative sitting solutions, often the chairs without a back, this was probably done partly to signal a dynamic style of management and an anti-authoritarian attitude. Are the days when chairs were important signs of authority over?

How functional was functionalism?

As far as furniture for sitting is concerned, there are grounds to query whether the twentieth century's functionalism really did lead to more functional solutions for the user – the sitting human being. The new pieces got rid of a lot of unnecessary ornamentation and detail, and they certainly became simpler to manufacture and easier to clean. However, the basic concept of sitting was not subject to review. With a few notable exceptions, the focus was not on the needs of the human body while sitting. In this sense, most of the furniture produced in the functional era was not more functional than the styles it replaced. Remember that concepts like the rocking chair and tilting work chairs for offices were not created by the functionalists, but in the nineteenth century.

Nor was the Scandinavian Design movement in furniture design, to which I feel a close affinity in many ways, particularly concerned with the needs of the sitting human body. Qualities such as aesthetics, function, honest use of materials, attractive details, etc. were given equal weight. In many places where furniture is needed, the quality criteria of Scandinavian Design are still the best, but in areas of application where we sit over a long period of time, these qualities do not fulfil our physical needs.

The stylistic ideals for furniture for residential sitting that have come in the wake of functionalism have not managed – or even tried – to respond better to the needs of the human body. Neither the low sitting arrangements with an abundance of soft cushions nor the static minimalist chairs designed for sitting at a high table represent any major move towards a more body-friendly philosophy.

Learning from the first long-term sitters

Modern society results in many of us having to sit on chairs in order to get our work done. The sitting posture has historical roots based on selected social and cultural ideals. How might things have been different if we had turned to history and learned from earlier eras' "long-term sitters"?

In the past, too, there must surely have been people who had to sit while they worked, apart from the small elite group of authorities who sat in central positions of power. Is there anything we can learn from these people when designing sitting devices for today and for the future?

Riders, whether they rode oxen, donkeys, camels or horses, are undoubtedly among the earliest long-term sitters. Riders always sit with a good posture and a well-balanced upper body. However, the saddle was not a source of inspiration for chairs for factory workers. Indeed, even motorcyclists sit in a slumped posture, because the pedals are in "the wrong place", unlike the horse rider's stirrups.

Sculptures of people rowing river boats in days of yore reveal that the rowers alternated between sitting and standing. Monks sat at angled tables with their thighs sloping downwards. However, with the advent of the industrial revolution, it was not these groups of workers who were used as models for work postures and the shaping of the office chair. Instead, middle-class dining chairs were chosen as the prototype.

Since monasteries were probably among the first places where people sat for extended periods of time for the purpose of working or learning, it is perhaps not so strange that Benedict of Nursia (480–547) compiled guidelines for the postures monks should assume.

While the congregation stood in churches until after the Reformation, the clergy, several hundred years earlier, felt the need to sit. They could easily have fixed this problem by installing stools, benches or chairs, but they chose not to do so. Instead they constructed an advanced sitting system with a hinged seat, known as a misericord. These chairs were constructed for three different body postures: in addition to sitting on a flat seat, the hinged seat could fold up against the wall exposing a saddle-formed seat that gave support when used half-sitting, half-standing in the stall. The third posture was standing, with the option of leaning forearms on support plates situated on either side of the seat.

What seems utterly amazing is that at that time, they not only designed the physical solution, i.e. the seat, but also – after the congregation was given the opportunity to be seated – they achieved variation of posture by reorganizing the time spent in church through the now-familiar church rituals.

Rowing a river boat, varying between sitting and standing.

Coachmen's seats sloped forwards, and there were footrests at several different levels in front of the driver.

The way in which sitting was organized in churches in the Middle Ages is in concord with the philosophy that has come into fashion during the last decade. If we had learnt our lesson from our elder forbears, things might have been very different today.

Rituals – the solution to an ergonomic problem?

"Please, take a seat!" is one of the first things we say when we receive a visitor – at work or at home. Perhaps we should introduce more variety into these "rituals"? "How about starting the meeting with a walk?" "Please, lie down!" "Let's talk at the standing table".

Church rituals were developed requiring worshippers to alternate between different bodily postures and thus provided the opportunity for movement and variation that facilitated getting through the long service: standing to sing, kneeling to pray...

When I was a child, we had to stand up when the teacher entered the room, when we were asked about our homework and when we had to recite a poem or read something aloud. We also stood to sing. This tra-ditional alternation bears witness to the fact that the need for a variety of movements and changes in bodily posture was widely understood in the past, and indeed up until quite recently.

There is a movement now in occupational ergonomics to reintroduce "rituals" in order to bring back some of the movement and variation our bodies need. For example, the photocopier, coffee machine and fax can be placed a good distance from the workplace (nor-mally the desk). This may seem like a sensible solution, but what is to be done about the extra irritation that is bound to arise as a result of these self-imposed incon-veniences when one is in a hurry? The disadvantages may well outweigh the advantages. Are roundabout remedies really the best we can come up with?

The secret may lie in the added advantages that result from the introduction of new, varied routines. For example, if industry went back to the system that required people on the assembly line to go personally to fetch the parts they needed from the storeroom, they would have the opportunity both to move a little and to have more varied social contact. Is it possible that this may, in return, increase our comfort and efficiency more than any automated or unilateral process could?

We may be more inclined to accept the following minor "inconveniences" at work: files can be placed on a high shelf so we have to stand up and stretch to get them; the telephone can be put on a high counter so that phone calls are made standing up.

On a more fundamental level, can we actually impose new routines on modern people, as was possible in the Middle Ages when the Church wielded sufficient authority to implement new codes of conduct? The best solution would be if the tasks we have to perform and our material surroundings themselves inspired us to use our bodies in more varied ways.

Are our lifestyles changing us physically?

Our friend and ancestor the ape has much stronger and longer arms than we, as well as toes that can grip – allowing him to move easily from tree to tree. With the passing of time, we climbed down from the trees, spending more and more time on the ground, and eventually our legs became our primary means of motion. Our arms grew weaker, and our legs became longer and stronger. Major changes in lifestyle led to physiological changes. What I wonder is how this bodily evolution will continue? Which groups of muscles will be maintained and developed, and which will shrink and wither as a result of our present lifestyles?

We are currently in a situation where our lifestyles are changing extremely rapidly, and our bodies simply cannot keep up. Do we even want our bodies to adapt? During the last hundred years or so, our muscles have grown weaker, and we have grown taller. Will this tendency continue?

We must remember that our bodies were originally suited for hunting and gathering food. Are the minimal and often repetitive muscle operations required to use a computer mouse enough to keep our bodies in prime condition? Will the active index finger operating the computer mouse evolve and grow larger?

Can developments in technology be expected to encourage a more active lifestyle? Perhaps in a few years' time when we can talk to our computers, we can return to dancing as we work. Will we go full circle and actually liberate ourselves from our tools and return to a condition such as existed in the era before Homo habilis? I think not. Luckily, there will always be plenty of jobs that have to be performed physically by people, and that is why it is important that those of us who design tools understand the needs of the human body.

Arms bore the brunt of movement when our ancestors lived in the treetops. Life on the ground meant we had to start using our legs to get around.

29

Our feet and legs are our department of transportation and have the main responsibility for moving our body.

For those of us who have evolved into Homo sedens, what solutions can there be to the challenges described in chapter 1?

- one is to spend less time sitting;
- the other is to introduce more movement and variation of posture into our sitting.

Although the first solution is clearly preferable, it is only the second one that I have any capacity to influence in my profession as a developer of chairs and sitting devices.

Why movement?

Why aren't we happiest when we are able to avoid movement and remain still?

If standing still was the most comfortable posture, musicians or singers would stand as still as statues while performing, and people waiting for a train would look like still mime artists. Yet they don't; they move. On the train platform, the movements may be miniscule, such as a slight shifting of weight from foot to foot, while the artist on the stage feels the need for more motion.

We can walk for hours, but we get tired after only a few minutes if we have to stand still.

It is more tiring to stand and watch a procession than to be part of it.

Our muscles are designed for dynamic use and are not well adapted to static strain. We soon feel discomfort if we have to keep our whole body or parts of our body still for any length of time. It is less tiring for us to use our muscles. If our muscles are not allowed a certain degree of activity, they send signals to our nerve centre that informs us that we are uncomfortable. This tells us something about basic needs that are not being satisfied. Inadequate blood circulation may be one of the reasons for these signals.

Why movement? The answer is simple.
We very often have the option of standing stock still, but we never do so.

Try holding one arm stretched out at a right angle to your body and keeping it still, while at the same time you bend and stretch the other arm.

Which arm gets tired first?

Movement is a beautiful word
When we want to express our feelings, we move. When we try to change something in society, we form a movement. We move to show strength, to express sympathy, to protest or to celebrate.

We move physically, we respond to kinaesthetic impulses by moving, we can be moved emotionally, and we get together and organize mass movements – for environmental awareness, human rights, etc.

Oscillations

Inanimate objects and living beings alike have inherent and natural oscillations according to which they reverberate. A familiar example is the tuning fork, with exactly 440 oscillations per second. If you strike a number of wine glasses, you will find that each glass has its own individual rate of oscillation. Trees in the forest sway to different rhythms; the elephant and the mouse each have their own biorhythm or oscillation, etc.

Man is no exception to this rule and also follows certain rhythms, oscillations or intervals. Intervals of activity and rest constitute one example of an inherent biorhythm. There is a longer oscillation between workdays and days of rest, and a shorter one between day and night. In the course of the day, we need to alternate between work and breaks, but the most neglected oscillation is that between active and relaxed use of muscles. Ideally, we should be alternating between actively using our muscles and relaxing them all the time, during all our various activities. This happens when we walk or run: the muscles alternate between activity and rest with each step we take. Because the leg muscles work dynamically, we can walk for a long time without resting.

Whether we can fulfil the body's need for dynamic use or not obviously depends largely on what kinds of activities we are engaged in, on our ability to listen to the signals our bodies send us and on how well our physical environment is adapted to this oscillation. The longer oscillations mentioned above are provided for in society, but the need to alternate between activity and relaxation while we sit is often neglected. Should we attempt to adapt devices for sitting to the natural oscillations of human beings – neither too rapid, nor too slow?

Why variation?

Isn't it a luxury to be able to stay put in our favourite posture for an hour or two?

When we place ourselves in our favourite posture on our favourite mattress for the night, if lying still in a single position was most comfortable for our bodies, surely we could expect to wake up in the morning in exactly the same position in which we fell asleep the night before? But this is never the case. We choose to leave even the most comfortable positions after a short while, and we turn over a surprising number of times during the course of a good night's sleep.

Try to imagine that you are caught in an avalanche and are buried in snow. The position you assume may be comfortable – your entire body is perfectly supported in every way, but how long will this remain comfortable? The mere idea of our arms and legs being stuck in one position is unbearable. Being forced to stay put in one posture is a recognized means of torture.

Perfect support for our bodies in the same posture is not the key to comfort. We are happy when we can switch between different positions, and it is unnatural for us to stay put in the same position for any length of time. Similarly, varied tasks are better for us than repeating the same operation over and over again for a long period of time.

This general human need for variety also applies when we are sitting. Although, of course, some bodily postures are more natural for us than others, it is pointless to ask what the best posture for our bodies or the best way of sitting is. Having held any posture for a while, the best posture is always the next one. Even the most "correct" way of sitting recommended by the most prominent experts becomes uncomfortable after a while.

The opposite of variety is monotony. In every sense, physical and mental, literal and figurative, variety is positive and monotony is negative.

After just a few minutes in a seat on an aeroplane or train or in the cinema, we start trying to find variation and new postures.

Even the most comfortable position in the most comfortable bed becomes uncomfortable after a while. Have you ever woken up with your arms around your partner?

Bodily impulses and psychological obstacles

Imagine that you are the guest of honour at some kind of formal, official ceremony and have to sit on a chair on stage in full view of everyone. How would you sit? You would probably sit in the way that etiquette dictates: for example, with your legs together and your upper body upright.

Then, when you get home after the reception and you are alone, you draw the curtains and lock the door. You pick up the newspaper and sit down. What kind of sitting posture would you adopt now? I doubt it would be the same one you used on the stage. In this kind of situation, most people forget the etiquette codes and follow the impulses their bodies. The chances are that you would arrange your limbs in an "uncivilized" manner, one that feels good to you.

We constantly receive impulses from the body, and most of these impulses are desires for change: i.e. fatigue = desire to sleep, hunger = desire to eat, cough = desire to clear the throat, etc. It might be taking things a little far to say that our bodies are always right, but I think our bodies know best when they ask us to make a change.

However, we don't always heed the signals our bodies send us asking us to change posture. Why is that? One reason may be that performing certain tasks makes it impossible, or that our physical surroundings prevent us from moving. But that is not the whole picture. The kind of movements we are "allowed" to make varies geographically, varies according to what kind of profession we're in, varies in different situations, varies with social class, etc. The power of the body's signals is challenged by the power of social habits and the norms of civilization.

The term "civilized" can mean a lot of things. One meaning is a learned pattern of conduct, as opposed to a natural, "untamed" type of behaviour: the more of the behavioural traits of the ape we remove, the

more civilized we become. All civilizations have codes or norms of conduct that are deemed appropriate or "civilized" in various social milieux or settings. These codes of good conduct apply to bodily postures and movements as well. For instance, try to imagine a group of American lawyers starting a meeting by giving each other massages, as is the norm when people meet in certain places in the Orient.

We are better at listening to and following our bodily impulses when we are children than once we have grown up, on informal occasions than on formal occasions, in our private spaces than in public spaces, and when we're tipsy or high than when we're sober. However, these impulses to change posture and move are the body's way of making the brain execute an action that the body needs in order to function optimally. If we listened to more of these impulses and followed them to a greater extent, we would move more freely and use postures that are more natural to us. As long as you are not causing harm or distress to anyone in your immediate surroundings, surely it is worth trying to follow the advice your body gives you?

Bodily impulses and physical obstacles

After roughly half an hour in the cinema, our bodies start to tell us that it is time to change position. Shouldn't the design of the seats take these bodily desires into consideration?

The back of a chair can be experienced as a physical obstacle by a person seated behind it. The drawings show that the person nevertheless tries to cope positively with the back of the chair in front in order to get some variety of position. Some pommels placed as footrests on the back of the chair would have made this person's seating more comfortable.

Although rules of etiquette and customs can impede us from following the signals our bodies send us, physical obstacles represent an even greater hindrance. In many professions it is impossible for people to follow many of their bodily impulses, as the machines or tools they use determine and restrict the body's movements. For instance, crane operators and cashiers at retail checkouts are not free to follow all the signals their bodies send them. For other professional groups, such as miners or car mechanics, it is the circumstances in which they have to perform their work that prevent the body from adopting natural postures.

Another obstacle to our behaving according to the wishes of our bodies is the demand for efficiency – or work pressure. If there is a long queue of people waiting for your services, you are hardly going to get down on the floor to do some stretches – regardless of the messages your body is sending you.

In terms of design challenges related to assuring the comfort of the human body, an important rule of thumb appears to be: allow the body to decide

for itself as far as possible in terms of the desire for changes in posture. Rather than giving the body a hard time, forcing it to try to adapt to the whims of the designer, it must surely be the designer's job to make it as easy as possible for people to follow the signals of their bodies – and perhaps even inspire them to do so.

In a certain type of aircraft, mechanics discovered that the varnish was continually being worn off at a certain part of the control panel on which there were no instruments. This applied to all aircraft of this type. A closer investigation of the matter revealed that this was the only space where pilots could put their feet up. In aircraft that did not have this instrument-free space, the pilots had no opportunity to follow the body's impulse for this kind of variation. As an aside, it must be noted that of all workspaces, that of the aircraft pilot is probably the most scrupulously and thoroughly planned.

39

The chairs we "wear"

Very few people today live in the natural environment without some form of shell or shield that provides protection and support. The human body is soft and dynamic, whereas the buildings or structures we have built for ourselves have to be hard and static so as not to collapse. The surroundings that are closest to human beings must take this quintessential difference into account: people are dynamic beings, not static entities. So how can we best design our surroundings?

First, we can start by questioning how close to the body we want the transition from the dynamic to the static to be. We certainly would not like it to happen on the surface of our skin. The body is flexible, and we like our clothes to be flexible, too. However, in addition to our clothes, most of us spend a lot of time "wearing" a chair of some sort – often for as long as 80% of our waking hours. Both at home and in many workplaces, these chairs that are in such close contact with our bodies are generally as static as the rigid structures that make up rooms and buildings.

What I am suggesting is that the chairs we "wear" for long periods of time should be neither as soft and flexible as our clothes, nor as hard and inflexible as our buildings. The chair should instead work as an intermediary between the dynamic body and the static architectural surroundings. If our clothes are our second skin, we could say that chairs have now become our third skin, and, similarly, that architecture and perhaps also cars and other vehicles are our fourth skin. Moreover, we have to take this into consideration when we design and build chairs intended for use over long periods of time.

A piece of furniture that is in contact with our body for long periods of time should adequately support the various parts of the body that need support, while also catering to the body's need for freedom, movement and variation. To achieve this, I am proposing that the dynamic area around the body be expanded at the expense of the static one.

Stiff clothes made of wood or steel will never gain widespread popularity.

Although initially there may not appear to be any direct link between standing on a surfboard and sitting in a chair, many of the same criteria actually apply to choosing a work chair as to choosing an item of sports equipment, i.e. the user needs to have optimal control and the ability to steer the item. Neither a chair nor a board should control you. The same goes for skating and skiing – the feet control the instrument, and balance facilitates movement. One of the reasons why we enjoy sports that involve equipment is our pleasure at being able to master or gain control over the tool, and I hope users will have a similar experience when mastering the tilting of the chair.

As you may see in sports, the skill is to find balance and obtain control.

Balance

Being in balance gives us control.
Being in balance inspires movement.

What is the best starting point for making a movement such as a step, a jump, or a lift?

Being well balanced is a prerequisite for effortless
movement.

When we lean against a wall or a support of some
sort, we can only remain still for a few minutes before
feeling discomfort. If on the other hand we stand
freely, and are balanced, we always choose movement, shifting our weight from one foot to the
other, pacing to and fro, etc.

The body is best able to respond
positively to any impulse to
move when it is in balance.
This happens automatically
while we are standing, but
does it also happen when
we are sitting? When
we sit upright on a stool
without a backrest, at least our upper bodies remain
balanced, but if we want our whole body to be in
balance, chairs must be designed expressly for this
purpose.

When a person sits in a chair, the tilting point should
be located beneath the body's centre of gravity.

It is this principle of balance that I use when the goal
is to allow and even encourage movements between
different postures.

*Being in equilibrium, physically as
well as mentally, is a good feeling.*

Foot control

The feet – the ignored extremities in ergonomics
Which parts of our anatomy control most of our movements? The answer is our legs and feet.

Our legs and feet have prime responsibility for moving us in almost all situations. When our ancestors moved down from the trees and started living on the ground, it was natural that the legs and feet became their main agents of transport. When we walk, run and jump, it is our legs and feet that control and execute the movements. Try turning over in bed without using your legs!

It seems only natural to me, therefore, that we should try to make sure that the legs can continue to handle this task when we are sitting in a chair.

Sitting on a chair balancing over the tilting axis, any displacement of the feet or body weight will provide movement to a new angle.

Ergonomists have tended to be primarily concerned with the upper parts of the body: the back, neck, shoulders and arms. The importance of the legs and feet to a person's sense of well-being and the tasks and needs of the legs while we sit have not been an area of particular focus in ergonomics.

Why do feet play such a key role in dynamic ergonomics? Because most of the major movements we make are governed by our "pedestrian extremities".

The feet and blood circulation
After a long flight during which our feet have not had much opportunity to move, our shoes can start to feel tight, because too much blood has gathered there.

Why do we want to move our feet to music? Is it just to follow the beat – a mere kinaesthetic response – or might it be because active footwork is conducive to better blood circulation? The heart does not suck blood back in from the body, it pumps it out. Movement and use of muscles, especially in the legs and feet, help bring the blood back to the heart. For example, when we move our ankles, the muscles we use act almost like a second heart.

In my dynamic chairs, the feet control the tilt angle, and this prompts the feet to change position constantly. This frequent and dynamic use of the leg muscles facilitates blood flow to the brain as well as production of synovial fluid, making both the brain and the body function better. This is the opposite of most tilt concepts used in work chairs, where the feet have less control, or no control at all, and have been made passive.

You can read more about this in Stranden's study, published on our website: www.opsvik.no/media/Stranden_Ergonomics_2000.pdf

chapter 3
favourite postures

Each part of the body has its favourite positions, but exactly which one is preferred at any given time is dependent on the positions the other parts of the body have assumed. The extent to which bodily parts can have their "desires" fulfilled depends on freedom of mobility and opportunities for support.

The feet

When we sit on the ground or the floor, it is what we do with our legs that most markedly distinguishes the various sitting postures from one another as shown previously under "sitting postures". For example, when sitting on the floor to have a meal in a Japanese restaurant, the main problem is what to do with our legs. The main functional reason that we sit on elevated levels, stools or chairs is undoubtedly that it allows our legs and feet freedom on a lower level than the one at which we are sitting.

Each of the angles or positions our upper body assumes when we sit has its appurtenant "favourite position" for the legs.

When we rest our upper bodies in a reclined position, we want to have our feet raised.
When we are active, leaning our upper bodies over a table, we want our feet low.

The reason that the seats of easy chairs and sofas are lower, making the floor seem higher, must be to ensure that we feel comfortable in a reclined position because we can place our feet on the relatively high floor level.

Normal seat height is approximately 45 cm for chairs intended for use at a standard table that is approximately 72 cm high. This is a comfortable combination when we sit upright, but if we want to lean over a table to concentrate on something in front of us, we would be more comfortable if there was a hole in the floor to accommodate our feet. Generally, there is no such hole, and as a second best solution, we often pull our feet back under the seat of the chair. The opposite happens when we lean back into a well-reclined position. Our natural inclination is to stretch our legs out in front of us and rest our feet on, or push our feet against, a higher surface than the floor.

These examples illustrate the extremes, but if you take a moment to test them out, you will probably find that your feet harbour some fairly unconventional "desires". It is important to take the feet's natural

Where do we want to put our feet?

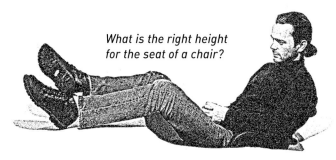

What is the right height for the seat of a chair?

desires into consideration when designing or buying furniture and when planning workplaces. Foot supports of various heights can be advantageous, as long as they do not hamper the free movement of the feet.

See pages 132–141.

In order to use a single standard table height and still enjoy our feet's favourite positions, the floor needs to have steps.
See page 136.

In order to be able to have your feet on the floor in all their favourite positions, the seat of the chair has to be adjusted up and down.

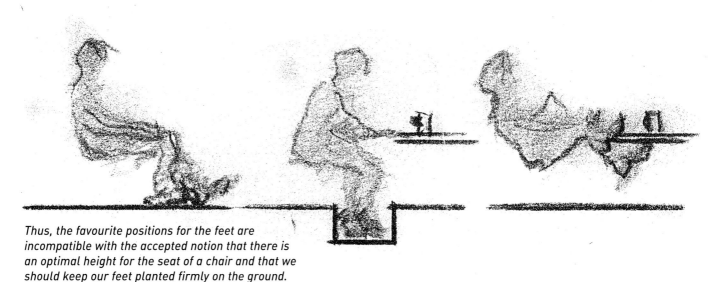

Thus, the favourite positions for the feet are incompatible with the accepted notion that there is an optimal height for the seat of a chair and that we should keep our feet planted firmly on the ground.

The middle regions

Moving upwards a little to the middle regions of the body, we might ask if they also have their favourite postures? Although the main message in this book is that there is no single posture that is always right or always wrong, I do believe, of course, that it is important to avoid overusing postures that put an unnecessary strain on the body. Take the spine for example. I believe that the spine is happiest when it can adopt the natural curvature that it has when we stand upright.

Our locomotive system is made up of a number of mechanical movable joints. When we try to fold the body into the traditional sitting posture with the hips, knees and ankles all bent at 90 degree angles, our ankles and knees are quite happy to bend at right angles. However, in most people, the hip joint stops bending after approximately 60 degrees and we make up the remaining degrees by straightening the curvature of the spine.

The traditional solution for being able to sit at a 90-degree angle and maintain the natural curvature of the lower back was for the chair to have a backrest that supported the lumbar region, ensuring that we maintained the natural curve of the spine. However, in practice, this does not work over extended periods of time. When we lean our upper bodies against the backrest, we have a tendency to slide forwards on the seat pan, thus straightening out the curve.

The following is an extract from A. C. Mandal's website: www.acmandal.com

Experts from all over the world have formerly been of the opinion that the proper sitting position is the right angle or erect position. The erect posture looks very nice, but it is impossible to sit this way for long and there is no scientific basis for it. It is entirely based

on wishful thinking, morals and discipline from the days of Queen Victoria. This erect sitting posture cannot be maintained for more than one or two minutes, and it usually results in fatigue, discomfort and poor posture.

In 1962, the German orthopaedic surgeon, Hanns Schoberth, demonstrated by x-ray photos that in a seated work position, you can only bend about 60 degrees in the hip-joints, not 90 degrees as shown in the drawings in fig.1. This means that when moving from a standing (lordosis) to an upright sitting position, you bend the hip-joints about 60 degrees and rotate the pelvis axis backwards, flattening the lumbar-curve (kyphosis) of the back 30 degrees and straining the muscles of the back. When leaning forward over the desk, you have to bend another 40–50 degrees, and this bending mainly takes place in the 4th and 5th lumbar discs. Even the best lumbar support will hardly have any influence on the posture when leaning over the desk.

If we sit actively and are constantly switching between different postures it is possible that this slumped posture described by Mandal is no more negative for the body than any other sitting posture. However, leaving your torso slumped like this for an extended period of time puts *a huge strain on the vertebrae*. This posture also renders us passive, as opposed to sitting with a balanced spinal column, a posture that inspires us to move as nature intended and thus builds up the supporting muscles.

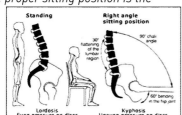

So, if most of us are unable to bend our hip joint sufficiently when sitting upright on a horizontal seat, and if we are unwilling to develop our muscles to do the job, the obvious question is how should we sit if we want to protect our lower backs?

Standing · Right angle sitting position · 30° flattening of the lumbar region · 90° chair angle · 60° bending in the hip joint · Lordosis Even pressure on discs · Kyphosis Uneven pressure on discs

As you have no doubt already concluded, the answer is to sit with a more open angle in the hip-joints. There are two ways of achieving a wider angle between the torso and the thighs:
- Either you have to slant your upper body backwards,
- or you have to sit with your thighs sloping downwards.

Slanting the upper body backwards
The angle between the thighs and the torso is then wide enough to reduce the harmful strain on the vertebrae, as long as there is adequate support for the back.

In cars, this posture rules supreme. A relaxed, reclining position with the hips at an open angle is in fact a good solution. However, this position does have some disadvantages; for instance, it is not especially practical as a working posture, as most of our work is generally performed at a table or with a machine in front of us. Furthermore, if supported in this posture for too long a time, the back muscles may be made passive. This is not the best position for the neck and shoulders, either.

Sitting with a vertical or forward-leaning torso and your thighs sloping downwards
A posture like this makes it easier for us to sit, with a balanced upper body and a natural curve in the spine without any back support.

Of course, you can sit with your thighs sloping downwards on any chair, if you perch on the edge of the chair and put your feet under the seat. But for this posture to be more comfortable and natural, the chair – or at least the chair's seat – requires a slightly different design.

Forward-sloping seat
One solution is to design the seat of the chair so that it can be tilted to slope forwards a few degrees.

A danger of course is that if the seat slopes forwards too much, the sitter will slide off the seat. So if you want to sit at a steeper angle, which of course is good for your back, there must be some means of preventing you from sliding forwards. To do this, I use two different solutions.

Shin rests
The first solution is shin rests, which are used in all my chairs that have the word balans in the name. Using shin rests allows the user a steeper downward slope for the thighs but without the risk of sliding off the seat. This means that it is easier to retain the natural curvature of the lumbar region.

Saddle-shaped seat
My second solution is to get the sitter to "ride" on a seat resembling a saddle, which has been adapted for use in the HÅG Capisco, "the saddle chair". When you sit in a saddle, it is impossible to slide off, even if your thighs are positioned vertically. This means that on this kind of seat, the sitter can assume the thigh angle that is desired and most comfortable, from horizontal to vertical.

However, in the case of a sitter assuming a posture with a high degree of downward slope of the thighs, the advantages for the back may come at a price that must be paid by other parts of the body. In order to prevent the user from sliding forwards, there must necessarily be pressure on the part of the body that acts as a brake to stop the sliding motion. If you sit on the edge of a chair, the ridge will dig into the underside of the thigh. Shin rests put pressure on your shins, and the saddle chair may exert pressure on the inside of the thighs. Although this pressure on the shins and thighs can be felt, one should be reminded that these are relatively uncomplicated parts of the body, when compared with the spine. The best way to avoid discomfort from the pressure placed on these parts of the body ("the brakes") is to change position frequently, and it is at this point that you will begin to appreciate a seat that easily tilts back to a horizontal or reclined angle.

Benefits to the back are not the only factors that impel us to sit with downward-sloping thighs and a more natural curvature of the spine. This posture is also beneficial for the neck and shoulders, and it provides better arm sweep and more space for the stomach and internal organs, which in turn ensures easier and deeper breathing.

The Norwegian physician Henry Seyfarth and the German ergonomist Ulrich Burandt developed chairs with a seat that could be tilted forwards, but the credit for so many workplaces now having chairs with seats that can be tilted forwards must go to the Danish physician A. C. Mandal, who has tirelessly advocated these theories concerning posture through his products, lectures and books.

Hans Chr. Mengshoel initiated the Norwegian experiments on sitting devices with supports under the shins, and this resulted in the design of many chairs with shin rests. For me personally, it has been important to consider kneeling as just one of several postures that can be assumed in a chair.

When we stand upright, most of us have a natural curve in the spine.

The sharper the angle between the upper body and the thighs, the more the natural curve of the spine is straightened out. When we lean forwards over our work in front of us, our spine will most likely be bent in the wrong direction.

The torso

The upper body is also generally most comfortable while we are standing, so it is probably safe to assume that this upright posture ought to be the upper body's favourite position, also when we are sitting, assuming that the lower body provides a good "open angle" permitting this posture.

But, what posture does the upper body prefer when we sit on a normal dining room chair? One thing is certain: we seldom sit with the upper body in conformity with the backrest angle that is typical for this type of chair.

When we sit down and lean back against the backrest of a chair, we may sit with a relatively upright upper body for a few minutes, –

– but we soon realize that in order to rest comfortably, the upper body needs to adopt a much greater angle of backward tilt than most chair backs are designed to provide.

The other favourite posture in this kind of chair is the complete opposite, with the upper body leaning forwards and our elbows resting on the table.

A third commonly used sitting posture is to lean the upper body sideways against a support. For example, we usually sit at one end of the sofa if we can, because it also provides us with side support.

Arms and hands

When we are seated, our arms require both freedom to move and lots of opportunities for support. Why do our arms need support?

- To ease the load placed on the back by the weight of our arms and hands.
- If we are to use our hands to carry out an activity, some form of support can in many cases reduce the strain on the muscles that results from holding our hands in the area where the activity is to be carried out.
- Having support for our hand and underarm can also provide more strength and precision for the work that is to be done.

A topic that is discussed is to what extent the arms should be supported when doing various tasks. Too much support can also lead to passivity, and can be detrimental. There are design solutions where arm supports are suspended from above by using cords, giving the seated person a puppet-like appearance. These are controversial.

When we sit, we try instinctively to find a place to put our arms, and if we don't find another place, we rest our arms on our laps. If we are sitting in a chair, there are more options, and if the chair has armrests these are of course a natural place to find support. We like to have the support vertically beneath our shoulders, and this means that when we rest our forearms on the tabletop, this is not only to give our arms a break; it also takes body weight off the back.

The top of the backrest is also ideal as arm support and one of the reasons my higher chairs have separate neck rests is to maintain the possibility of using the backrest as an armrest.

The head

The head is perfectly comfortable when it is balanced on top of a naturally curved, upright spinal column. However, if we have chosen to adopt a posture where the upper body is leaning strongly one way or the other, it is not so natural or easy for us to balance our heads. In these kinds of postures, we sometimes feel the need to support our heads, regardless of the angle of the upper body.

Since we bend the upper body forwards, it is relatively difficult to place physical devices that can support the head (see page 126), meaning that it is most convenient to rest our head in our hands. If we lean the upper body to one side or backwards, it is easier to find support for the head and neck on the support elements of the chair.

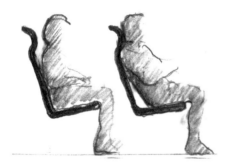

Traditional chairs that are designed to provide support for the uppermost part of the human body tend to have a solid plate-like backrest that rises from the seat to neck level with some form of protuberance at the top to support the neck. This is an ergonomically unfortunate solution for a number of reasons. A high-backed chair of this kind is very constrictive, and there is nowhere to put your shoulders and arms if you try to sit sideways in the chair. Another weakness is that it is impossible to get support for your neck and your lower back at the same time – the one is supported at the expense of the other. Because the shoulders are impeded by the compact backrest, the only way to achieve support for the neck is to move forwards in the seat and thus lose the support for the lumbar region.

My solution is to make sure that there is a gap between the backrest and neck rest to allow the shoulders freedom of movement. Just as pauses are important in music, gaps can be as important as support in furniture for sitting. When the backrest tilts, it does not simultaneously affect the position of the neck rest.

This means you can retain the support for the lower back while at the same time getting full support for the neck.

A space between the back support and neck support allows the user to sit sideways and use the top of the backrest as an armrest, and enjoy the same freedom as in a low-backed chair. He is not limited to only facing forwards when sitting, as is the case in conventional high-backed work chairs.

Chair profiles

Four body postures and three chair profiles.

Which of these three chair profiles provides the best support in all four postures?

The convex, the straight or the concave seat and backrest profile?

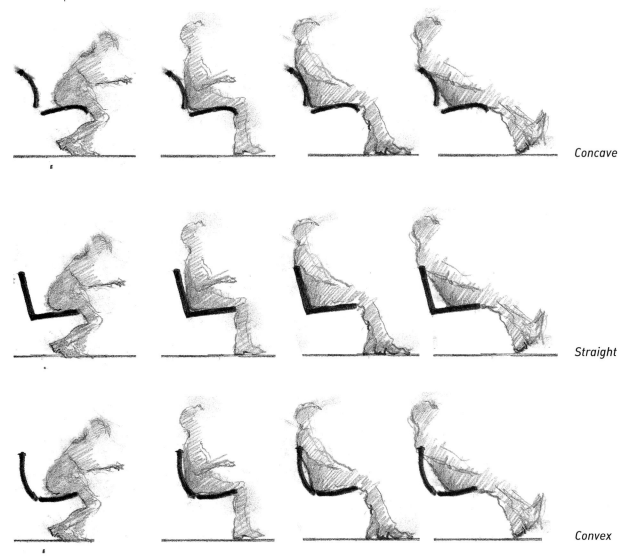

Concave

Straight

Convex

chapter 4
tilting – four concepts

Tilting – four concepts

In this chapter, I will demonstrate my own products as practical examples based on the theories expounded in the previous chapters. The advantages to the users that I hope these furniture items will provide are actually quite elementary; in principle, they are designed to give us a sense of well-being when we sit. A prerequisite for being able to enjoy sitting is to have the freedom to alternate between postures as often and as effortlessly as possible. The most common changes of posture while sitting in a chair are various sitting angles ranging from a reclined position to an active, forward-leaning position. This chapter shows four concepts which inspire the sitter to move and change postures from angle to angle, without thinking about it and without having to regulate the chair. The secret lies in the fact that one balances freely without any restricting locking mechanism.

The wheel

The balanced tilt

Spiral springs

Suspended from above

In chairs with curved runners, it is the runners' contact with the floor that constitutes the tilting point. Imagine placing a person inside a wheel, and that this person changes position inside it. The ball or the wheel has an exceptional quality: when rolling on a flat surface, it always comes to rest in a balanced position.

On the ground, there is no instrument that moves us more efficiently than the wheel. My intention for the rocking chairs has been to place the person "inside the wheel", as it were, imagining the runners as part of a wheel. In this case, however, the wheel is not circular; instead, it has a curve designed for both stability and motion. This is where my design differs from the traditional rocking chair.

The user balances directly above the point where the runner meets the floor. This is one of the simplest ways of creating tilting movements in a chair – and this in turn means that it should be simple to initiate movement.

Sitting in a rocking chair is a bit like sitting inside a wheel – the wheel easily generates movement.

A movement as small as the nodding of one's head or reaching out with an arm moves the centre of gravity enough to make the "wheel" start moving into a new sitting angle.

A pendulum upside down

Our two favourite postures at the table are shown in the illustrations below. We seldom sit in the upright manner that traditional chairs impose for us. We generally prefer to lean back or lean forwards. The Pendulum concept that I started working with in 1978 is an attempt to allow the chair to follow the natural inclinations of the body.

The chair tilts forwards and backwards from a normal position. On this kind of chair, the maximum possible forward angle of the upper thigh cannot be as steep as is attainable on a chair with shin rests or a saddle seat, but it is more favourable than on a seat that is fixed horizontally or tilted backwards.

The purpose of the long, slim backrest is to accommodate the largest possible number of sitting postures. In addition, it provides support if one sits sideways on the chair. The slim form of the backrest is intended to inspire users to "open" their chest regions by bending their shoulders back. The slim backrest also makes it possible to use the top rail as forearm support and in this way alleviate the weight of the arms and shoulders. If we sit leaning back, the natural support point for the forearm is alongside the backrest, not further forwards on the side, where traditional armrests are often placed.

Pendulum, STOKKE, 1983–2006 and VARIÉR, 2006–

Residential sitting

Comfort has not always been the main concern when designing chairs to be used at the dining table.

Many of my chairs are attempts at remedying this situation. One example is the Actulum. Sitting angles change when the entire chair tilts. In addition, the backrests tilt around the top stretcher.

Environmental ideas behind the Actulum

Function
This chair meets the body's need for movement and variation. A user that is used to sitting on a dynamic chair finds it very difficult to revert to a static one. For this reason alone, this chair limits the likelihood of the user buying another chair or replacing this one.

Materials
Wood is a renewable material. By using a laminated construction, maximum use is made of the wood by peeling it off to make veneer layers. The wood surface can be treated with bio-oil or wax.

Dimensions
The dimensions can be kept sleek because the laminated construction is strong. It can be packed flat for storage or transport.

Maintenance
Simple replacement of the less durable parts – the upholstery and the cushion – is easily done without the need for tools. If the cushions wear out, the chair can be used without cushions.

"Timeless"
The visual design will hopefully remain popular for many years, without appearing old-fashioned.

Areas of use
This chair can be used in all situations where people need to sit at a table, thus providing a range of second-hand, third-hand, etc. areas of use. For example, having served ten years at the main table in the home, the chairs can be dispersed and used separately as office/work chairs.

Actulum, STOKKE, 1995—2006 and VARIÉR, 2006-

Chair, 2003, prototype →

Seat + shin support

How many parts of the body need to be supported?
This simple chair has three supporting surfaces for the
body, while the larger chairs shown on the following
pages have supporting surfaces for a greater number
of parts of the body.

It is difficult to recommend the degree of complexity
that a piece of furniture designed for sitting should
have. This is dependent on many factors, but Variable
balans® may be the chair for cognizant users who like
to sit "actively" and find the proper equilibrium for their
upper bodies and heads. By sitting "actively", users
strengthen their back and abdominal muscles. It is the
muscles, rather than the spine, that bear the weight of
the upper body.

As the name *Variable* indicates, it is of primary
importance that the chair allows movement and
variation – the kneeling posture is one of many.
Like all other body postures, kneeling also
feels wrong after a while.

It is particularly when a person is performing activities on a table in front of
him that the small balans® chairs may
have an advantage over traditional chairs.
See pages 49–51.

*The two separate shin supports and the curved
runners faciliate switching between kneeling
and the more traditional posture.*

Variable balans®, STOKKE, 1979–2006 and VARIÉR, 2006–

Seat + shin support + back support

The curved runner is a simple and obvious medium for attaining movement and variation, even in the workplace. The chair can be adjusted for people whose height is 155 cm or more. The shin supports can be adjusted upwards and backwards, and the back support can be regulated forwards or backwards.

The key purpose of the adjustment is to be able to find the right balance point, so that tilting on the chair will inspire users to vary their sitting angle and posture.

What is the function of the backrest on a chair like this? The more variations in sitting postures that are attainable on a chair, the better, and Thatsit balans®, with the backrest, provides more variations than a chair without a backrest. Duo balans®, which additionally has armrests and a headrest, makes even more variations possible (see next page).

Of course, all of these chairs can also be used to balance an unsupported upper body. But being able to lean against the backrest on occasion is a welcome option.

Oposit balans®, STOKKE, 1988–1999

Thatsit balans®, STOKKE, 1991–2006 and VARIÉR, 2006–

Seat + shin support + back support + armrest + headrest

My intention was to design a chair that can function equally well for taking a light snooze as for working at the computer. Like all my runner-chairs, Duo balans's® angle is adjusted by the body's movements. Users can switch between the three main postures with slight shifts in body weight. The gap between the headrest and the tilting backrest provides space for freedom of movement for the arms and shoulders. Unlike conventional highback chairs, lumbar support actually increases in the reclining position.

Can a work chair look like this?

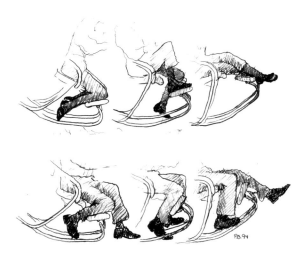

Being able to place our feet in different positions is essential for our well-being. It is also important that these foot supports do not slide away from us.

When we lean back against the backrest of a chair, we tend to slide forwards on the seat and thereby lose

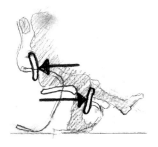

lumbar support. On many of my chairs, the shin rests can counteract this forward slide.

Duo balans®, STOKKE, 1984–2005

How many body postures on a single chair?

After resting for a while, we want to be active, and after being active for a while, we want to rest. Why can't we alternate between active and reclining body postures on one and the same chair?

Traditionally, people furnish their homes with one kind of furniture for resting and another kind for performing activities.

Gravity balans® has four positions or tilting angles, and in all of them the person sitting is so close to the balancing point that with the slightest shift of the body, the chair brings the user from one sitting angle to another.

"There's only one way to think clearly, and that's with your legs on the table. That way your blood goes to your head and not to your feet." (Tage Voss)

Gravity balans®, STOKKE, 1983–2006 and VARIÉR, 2006–

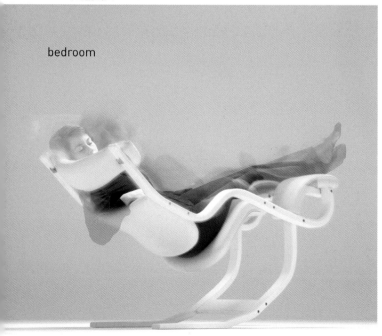

bedroom

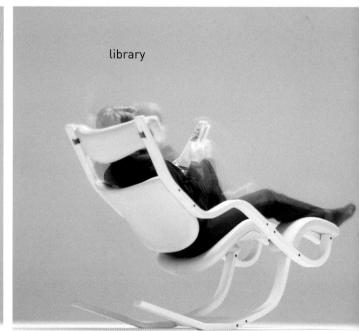

library

home office

dining room

Chair, 2006, prototype

Activities and relaxation

In living rooms, is it possible to "raise" and activate the seating that is now reserved for rest and relaxation so that it could also be suitable for performing activities at the table, such as having meals, or carrying out hobby work, homework, home office work, etc.? This may be especially relevant in small living units: you can sleep, read or watch TV in the same environment as the one in which you can have a meal or work.

The table needs to be high enough for the knees to fit underneath, but low enough to be accepted as a visual alternative to the low coffee tables that people are accustomed to.

The strap under the table is used as support for the feet and legs.

Chair, STOKKE, 1987

*Table, 1997, prototype
Chair, Tripos,
STOKKE, 1997–2002*

The balanced tilt, like my three other principles in this chapter, is highly advantageous since the user automatically controls the tilting movements of the chair without having to think about it. The user can concentrate on his/her activities and does not have to bother with mechanical regulation of the chair. The chair follows the natural inclinations of the body and automatically stabilises at the body's selected sitting angles or at the angles that are required by the work task being done. The simplest way of verifying this is to try out one of my chairs in front of a work table during a normal working day. What you will discover is that the chair tilts forward when you want to be active at the table and tilts backwards when, for example, you want to relax or talk on the telephone. You will also discover that these variations often occur many times per minute. Why does the tilting of the chair follow the user? Because the user is balancing.

The seat and back of the chair are joined to form what might be called the body of the chair. This moves freely from a forward-tilted angle to a reclining angle by tilting over a turning point or axis underneath the seat and at the very centre of the body's weight.

To change the angle of the tilt, we simply apply increased or decreased weight to the front of the seat and thereby start the tilting movement, or we ensure a stable angle for the chair. The position of the feet influences movement between postures as well as stopping and resting in the various positions. For example, to change quickly from a backward tilt or resting position to a forward-tilted, active position, simply stretch out or swing your feet under the seat. The pressure exerted by the thighs (or rather the weight of the legs) on the front of the seat will then help tip the body of the chair forward. To tilt backwards, lessen the pressure on the front of the seat and the body of the chair will tilt backwards.

Another example is that if we are sitting on an almost flat seat and require more backrest support, we can place a foot under the seat, thereby applying more pressure to the front of the seat and at the same time

It is a good feeling to be in balance and find equilibrium. Balance = control.

The fact that the front of the seat tilts up and down gives the feet the best possible control over the tilting angles of the chair.

increasing the pressure on the lumbar region. It is also possible to place one or both feet on the base of the chair, which will relieve pressure on the front of the chair seat and cause the body of the chair to tilt further back.

Tilting in balance with a seat front that goes up and down gives the user's feet and legs control over the chair's tilting movements, and therefore the feet are kept in constant activity. The advantage of this is that the frequent and dynamic use of the leg muscles ensures production of synovial fluid, and more importantly, this activity facilitates better blood circulation to the heart and brain. See www.opsvik.no/media/Stranden_Ergonomics_2000.pdf

The tilting concept of a work chair, the main trend

The goal of most designers of modern tilting work chairs has been to ensure that the tilting movement of the chair occurs without the front edge of the seat moving up or down. This is based on the apparently logical idea that the lower legs are of a fixed length – they are not made of elastic – and that the height from the floor to the top of the seat should therefore correspond to the length of the lower leg regardless of which tilted position the chair is in. As you have undoubtedly understood by now, I regard this tilting principle, which is by far the most commonly applied for work chairs, as a poor solution, particularly if we want the chair to respond easily to the user's needs. I shall explain why.

In a "knee-tilt" or "synchron mechanism" chair, the tilting point is placed under the front of the seat and most of the body's weight is therefore positioned behind the chair's tilting point and is kept in place by a spring. If the spring is taut enough to enable sitting upright with good lumbar support, tilting back to a reclining position can be more difficult. On the other hand, if the spring is slack enough to facilitate a comfortable backwards position, will these chairs be able to offer you a forward-tilted seat without locking the tilt? It can also be difficult to achieve a flat seat and at the same time good back support in an upright position without having to tighten the spring, or lock the chair in that position.

The user of a chair normally alternates between various sitting angles from one minute to the next throughout the day. The tilting mechanism used in these types of chairs lacks the capability to provide satisfactory support over this wide range of body postures when the chairs are equipped with only one mechanical setting.

As a result of this engineering dilemma, the user is faced with two choices:
* to sit uncomfortably in all other postures than the one for which the chair is regulated, or
* to mechanically regulate the chair's tilting resistance or to lock the angle between each change of position.

You will not be balanced over the tilting point, or fulcrum, and you cannot influence both sides of "the pair of scales", therefore you have limited control over the tilt. The positioning of the feet and the varying pressure of the thighs against the front edge of the seat will have little, if any, influence on the movements and angles of the body of the chair. You could even jump up and down on the front of the chair seat without the body of the chair reacting.

My general assertion is as follows: the user has poor control over the tilting movements of any chair that maintains a constant height for the front of the seat when tilting.

Since the feet do not determine the movements and the angles we want to sit in, this must necessarily result in more static sitting and less variation. After sitting in this kind of chair for a while, there is a risk that the feet and legs give up in their attempts to tilt and alter the sitting angle of the chair, thereby becoming stationary. In addition, these complicated "knee tilt" or "syncron tilt" mechanisms generate so much friction that you need to use force to initiate a tilting movement, whereas the nearly frictionless reaction of our "balanced tilt" design actually initiates movement.

"A chair for every position"

Credo was a response to the following considerations:
- a person's salary level should not determine the functionality of his chair
- we have not been created for a static life
- we come in different sizes

Credo's motto "a chair for every position" addressed not only body positions but also the hierarchical "positions" held in a commercial enterprise. In the past, it was primarily only the people holding a certain "position" who were privileged enough to have a chair that tilted, and these chairs only tilted backwards.

Credo was the first work chair to feature "free movement" from an active posture with a forward-tilted chair body, to a reclined posture with a backward-tilted chair body. The body's balance and the feet regulate and control the tilting movement.

Credo has a seat plate that slides forwards and backwards for regulating seat depth. I introduced this principle in the HÅG 2010 chair in 1975.

Most of the chairs I have developed for HÅG build on this tilting concept.

HÅG Credo, HÅG, 1984

HÅG H04 Credo, HÅG,
redesigned in 1992

Making it simple to get into balance

Like Credo, H05 is constructed on the principle that the user sits balanced above the tilting point and the placement of the feet controls the chair's movements and tilting angle. In addition to the tilt in the backrest, there is an automatic widening of the angle that occurs between the seat and the backrest when one tilts backwards in the H05.

Credo was the first office chair that tilted freely and comprised numerous ways of making adjustments to customize the chair to any body size. H05 is the first to make adjustments easy: it has one lever for height and a wheel that simultaneously adjusts seat depth, back height and tilting resistance.

Combined functions make it easy to achieve an ideal average setting. However, users can also choose their own "custom setting" by using the wheel to set the seat depth first. Users who are dissatisfied with the back height determined by the standard setting should adjust the backrest height separately. Users dissatisfied with the tilting resistance can tighten or slacken forward and backward tilt by using small "switches" while seated. We can compare this with a modern camera, which when set on automatic, takes good pictures on average but when set manually can take pictures with the specific effects one wants.

- easy adjustment for the casual user,
- lots of possibilities for individual adjustments for the discerning user.

Armrests often get in the way when they come into contact with the desktop. This chair is available with armrests that can be swung backwards out of the way. They remain behind the chair and function ideally as elbow rests when the user leans back.

← HÅG H05, HÅG, 2000– →

Initiating a movement is easiest when we are in balance. When we are in balance while sitting, we will change posture more often than when we are supported but are out of balance.

Our feet convey us in most situations in life. They are experts at moving us, which is why it is only natural that they should also be able to control our rocking or tilting movements while we are seated.

The ends of the bars of the swivel base are designed to be used as foot rests when you want to vary your sitting posture.

Chairs for general use

Many of the chairs shown in this book have in common that they can be used for different purposes and in different areas. This applies particularly to those shown on the next few pages, up to and including spiral springs.

Whether we sit at the breakfast table, at school, at our place of work or in a meeting, our pattern of movement and the postures we tend to adopt are largely the same. There is therefore no reason why chairs must be specially designed for different areas of use. These chairs fit anywhere where people are supposed to sit.

I hope that this intended flexibility will keep these chairs in use for a long time to come. There will always be new areas where these chairs can be useful, even if they have to be removed from the areas where they were originally meant to be used. For example, if you want to renew a set of dining chairs after ten years or so, the old ones can perhaps be taken over by the children – who are now perhaps in their teens – for doing their studies.

← *HÅG H05, HÅG, 2000–*

HÅG H05 Communication, HÅG 2002–

A simple solution

In view of how uncomfortable the chairs that are made available to us in the meeting rooms of the world's conference centres and hotels are, a proposal was made for a simple, lightweight chair that enables users to tilt forwards or backwards. I recommend that terms such as "meeting chair" or "conference chair" should not be used for products such as these because the denotations may prove limiting with regard to the areas of use for which the chairs are suited.

HÅG Conventio, HÅG, 1996–

Comfortable sitting without padding

When one sits dynamically and tilts the chair at different angles, the areas of pressure between one's body and the surfaces of the chair are distributed to different parts of the body and one thereby avoids the negative feeling of a "hard seat". Uncomfortable pressure on the sensitive spine may be avoided by the V-shape in the centre of the backrest; instead, the pressure will be distributed between the muscles on either side of the spine. It is important that the surface of the seat provides friction when it comes into contact with the seated person's clothes. Perforations or holes counteract stickiness.

Environment

The padding is the part of a piece of sitting furniture that is normally the first to wear out. Making a chair comfortable without using padding results in a longer service life for the chair. If one wants a chair with cushions, however, these are easy to replace with new ones as the originals become worn. As an alternative, one can continue to use the chair without cushions.

The seat and back of the HÅG Conventio are made from recycled car bumpers and household waste. The plastic components are labelled by type for at-source sorting. The chair consists of a small number of elements made from recyclable materials, which are easy to disassemble and replace.

See page 194.

At lengthy meetings, people appreciate being able to move and to vary their body postures.

Torsion in wood

The torsion concept expands the possibilities inherent in laminated wood's natural flexibility. It is well known, of course, that laminated wood constructions are supple and lend a certain amount of flexibility to chairs. This concept, however, brings with it completely new possibilities for movement, via a controlled-torsion twisting of laminated wood. Precise cut-outs create the desired dynamics in the back and seat of the chair.

As a rule, the technique behind traditional forward and backward tilting chairs is found in mechanical devices and mechanisms. With this new concept, laminated wood alone does the whole job.

- Cut-outs in the chair seat regulate the tilting motion and resistance of the entire chair.
- Cut-outs in the chair back allow yield in the upper back of the chair when pressure is applied. This provides better curvature and support for the lower back than it is possible to achieve with a traditional, laminated wood backrest without cut-outs.

→ *The cut-outs and characteristics of the tilting motion result in a tilting range of approximately 15 degrees backwards and 7 degrees forward, which would otherwise require some kind of mechanism to achieve.*

In musical string instruments, the f-hole notches on the top surfaces are designed to emit vibrations that produce sound; on the Viola, the notches are designed to produce vibrations in the human body in order to induce movement.

Viola, NATURELLEMENT, 2005–

Chair, 2003, prototype

Play with plywood

Chair parts cut out of flat plywood board may have a trim appearance, but they are normally quite uncomfortable for the sitter. By using the torsion principle, the plates yield in the right places, resulting in forward and backward tilt, as well as supporting curvature in the lumbar region. The chair requires little space when it is folded up and is a strong candidate for inclusion in chapter 6, which deals with size and space-saving.

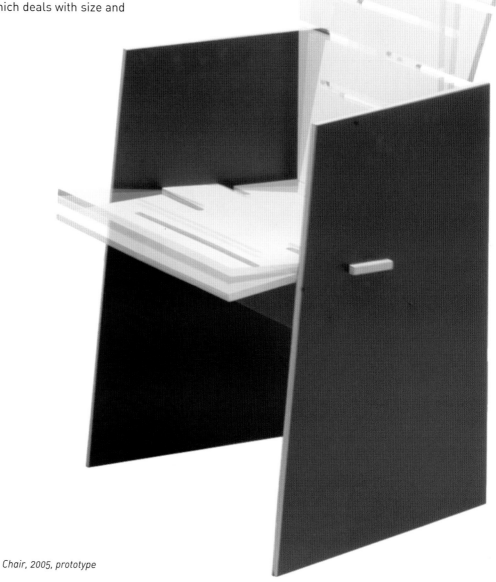

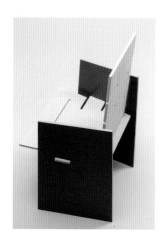

Chair, 2005, prototype

A laminated wood shell forms the seat and backrest. The transverse steel tubes are not fixed to the seat but are able to revolve, and the flexibility of the angled legs makes the chair tilt.

2002, prototype

Penguin, VARIER FURNITURE, 2008–

When one tilts backwards on a chair, the best resting areas for the forearms are on either side of the backrest; when one tilts forward, the table surface is a natural area of support. This is the reason why so many of my chairs have just such forearm supports.

Chair, 2002, prototype

According to this concept, the user sits "in a posi-tion to tip the scale" and is thereby inspired to shift posture. The tilting points are the point of contact between the four spiral springs and the floor.

The ergonomic benefits for the user are basically the same as in the other two concepts, but spiral springs provide a unique form of movement, mostly back and forth, but also sideways. The springs give the sitter the feeling that the body is liberated from the floor. It feels almost as if the chair is floating, and the chair responds instantly to the body's movements. Using spiral springs as a transitional mechanism between static and moving solutions has the added advantage that the chairs quickly and easily respond to the body's desire for very slight movements while we sit. They also provide a smooth transition between the different tilt angles.

Liberate the chair from its static surroundings

If you place your feet on the runners you will feel as if you are being released from the floor and floating on four coil springs. When the feet are placed on the floor, they command full control over the chair's angle of tilt.

Allow your feet to move you even after your have assumed a sitting posture.

Major movements become gentle.
Minor movements become buoyant.

The best condition for movement, or
for being moved, is to have balance.

Flysit, STOKKE, 1990–2000

4 wooden parts + 4 coil springs
provide a unique kind of freedom.

Motion, STOKKE, 1998–2003

The chairs or support surfaces are suspended from ropes.

What is it that fascinates us about sitting on a swing? It gives us a sense of freedom. No other kind of seat allows us such freedom of movement as one suspended from ropes. A pendulum clock can keep going for weeks on the small amount of force generated by the spring, proving the efficacy of this principle.

With this design concept it is particularly difficult to sit still. Perhaps such movements spark associations to the time when we floated effortlessly in the womb?

Almost impossible to remain static

No one ever sits completely still on a playground swing, do they? That's because we all prefer movement to remaining motionless when our surroundings are conducive to it. Suspended bodies move smoothly and rhythmically, responding easily to any influence. No other sitting device can so easily set us in motion as the playground swing.

The body of the chair hangs from two ropes that are fastened to the top of the C-shaped sidepieces. These attachment points are the chair's "tilting mechanism", allowing forward and backward tilt. These angular movements occur in addition to the floating swing movements on the horizontal plane. The height of the chair is adjusted by tightening the ropes. The seat and back plates are also attached with flexible bands to provide tilting.

The chair can also be suspended from the ceiling or a pyramid-shaped stand. Because the chair is suspended from a fixed point, it is recommended that it is only used with lightweight tables on wheels.

HÅG stand, Scandinavian Furniture Fair, 1986

Tilting forwards or backwards is possible without a resource-intensive mechanism

Prototypes displayed at the exhibition "Peter Opsvik – Movement" in Ghent, 1999

"It don't mean a thing
if it ain't got that swing"
Duke Ellington

"Keep on swingin'" also after sitting down.

HÅG Swing, HÅG, 2002–2007

Factor 10

In this concept I have tried to get a lot of movement out of minimal resources. Compared with traditional office chairs, we have done away with the base star, the lifting column and complicated tilting devices. The rope performs all of these functions and more. In addition, the materials are renewable wood. Initial studies show that the version of Swing that is suspended from the ceiling, without cushions, has only 1/10 of the environmental load of a comparable working chair. This "Factor 10" reduction in consumption of resources is necessary in industrialized countries in order to achieve global sustainability in the next 30 to 50 years.

Natural rhythm

Actually, this concept should not be placed under the category of "tilting". The motion in this concept functions in another way than what we normally associate with tilting movements. However, since the chairs fit well in the category of "suspended from above", they are included here.

I believe that we all have an internal rhythm that is constantly pulsating inside us, and that this rhythm should be able to express itself while we sit as well. When sitting in a suspended device, the slightest twitch of a muscle is enough to set the body in motion in a natural rhythm or frequency corresponding to the body's needs and requirements, physical as well as mental.

The seat, backrest and neck rest are suspended in such a way that they respond instantly to the desires of the body in terms of sitting angles and movement, as well as providing the necessary resistance and support.

Bulky padding materials are not necessary when the design itself ensures easy contact between the body and the support surfaces of the chair. We have thus achieved a high degree of comfort with a modest use of materials.

When sitting suspended, rhythm and frequency harmonize with the urges of the human body, both physical and mental.

Reflex1, NATURELLEMENT, 2002–

Reflex2, NATURELLEMENT, 2004–

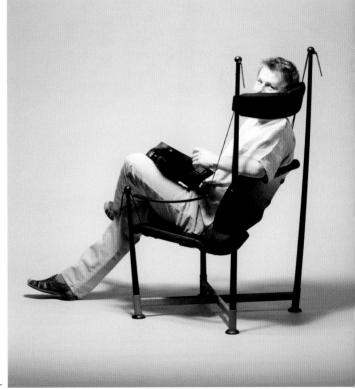

Conceptual arrangement of chairs whereby the bodies are in motion. Displayed at the exhibition "Peter Opsvik – Movement" in Ghent 1999, London, Glasgow, Gothenburg 2000 and Munich 2002. In this version, the message is more important than the functionality.

Hybrid

This chair is a hybrid and it could just as easily have been placed under the heading "The Wheel". Both its curved rails and its suspended support areas provide a floating sensation. The tilt angle depends on where you place your feet.

Reflex3, NATURELLEMENT, 2008–

chapter 5

support

rethinking sitting

Because of gravity, the human body has weight. The challenge to all forms of sitting furniture is to provide support so that we can assume the body postures we prefer.

In the previous chapter, support was also a topic, although movement was the primary focus. In this chapter, the questions addressed are: where do we want support? Where do we want freedom? And what shape should the support elements take?

Students work

After a few minutes in a chair, we begin to stretch out and try to lean backwards into a more comfortable posture. What we normally encounter is the rigid upper edge of the backrest, which from that point on becomes an inhospitable point of contact between our back and the chair.

During my student years, I tried to do something about this, and the following is the result. The plates in the seat and backrest are suspended between the back piece and front piece on textile strips, and they can be mounted in the frame in four different ways in order to create variation. The weight of the body against the seat plate provides adequate resistance when the top of the backplate is pressed backwards.

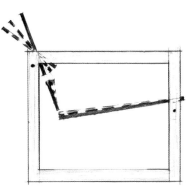

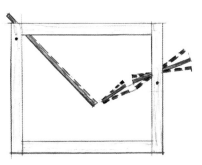

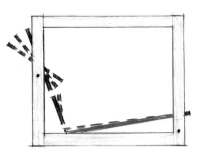

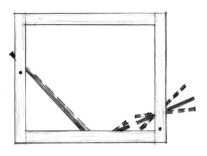

Diploma certification task, 1964

113

"Lay-out"

An attempt to remake a bed into a sofa with many
comfortable sitting and reclining positions.

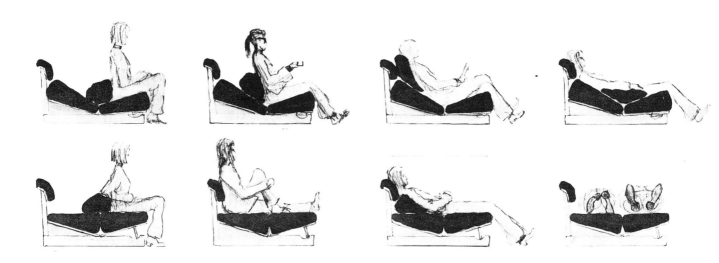

Lay-out, STRANDA INDUSTRI, 1968–1972

Liberation

Liberation from traditional furniture.

From an exhibition in the Norwegian National Association
for Applied Arts in Uranienborgveien 2, Oslo, 1970.
Fabrics: Gro Jessen

Balans®

At the end of the 1970s I embarked on a special experimental period, which is why a brief general history is in order.

A number of Norwegian designers felt the need to take an unbiased look at potential supportive constructions that the human body might find comfortable when assuming a seated posture. We started a series of experiments to rid ourselves of the stereotypical view of sitting and seating that we had grown up with. As I mentioned previously, A. C. Mandal and Hans Chr. Mengshoel were key sources of inspiration when the new thinking began.

Many of my experimental furniture designs from that time had a kneeling posture with support under the shins as one of many possible positions. It was Mengshoel who initiated the concept of the kneeling posture in Norway, and all of my chairs with shin supports and which have "balans" in their names originate from this initiative. Svein Gusrud, Oddvin Rykken and I were three designers who developed innovations in collaboration with Mengshoel, based on this principle. All four of us got help from the Norwegian Furnishings Manufacturers' Association to display home-made prototypes at our own stand at the 1979 Scandinavian Furniture Fair in Copenhagen.

Scandinavian Furniture Fair in Copenhagen, 1979

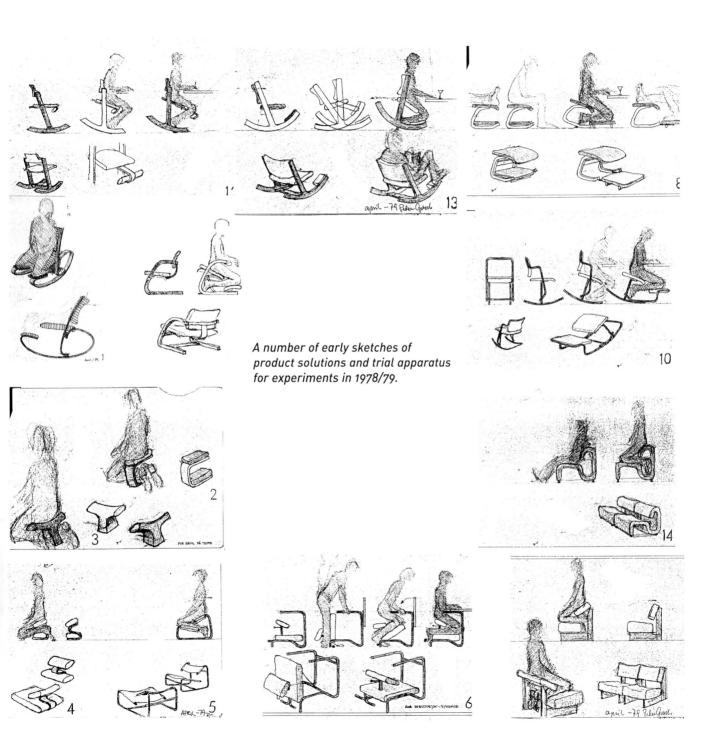

A number of early sketches of product solutions and trial apparatus for experiments in 1978/79.

Sitting unconventionally on a conventional chair

With its tilting backrest, this chair can provide proper support in many interesting sitting positions. When the angle of the upper body reclines so far back that holding the head up is strenuous, the headrest is in the right place to provide support.

If this chair, like most easy chairs, was equipped with a connected back support from seat to top, this sitting posture would be impossible.

balans® G-chair, RYBO, 1979–1985

Shin support rather than back support

The first thing a sitting device needs is a seat that keeps the body at a raised level. If an additional support unit is desired, this is usually in the form of a backrest. But is this always an appropriate option?

A person who has to carry out a lot of activities at his or her desk or table may benefit more from shin support than from a backrest.

This concept functions at different table heights, from normal desk heights and upwards, but is most comfortable when used with tables approximately 85–90 cm high.

→ *HÅG balans® Vital, HÅG, 1983–*
← *Wing balans®, STOKKE, 1983–2006 and VARIÉR, 2006–*

"I'm bringing my own"

This chair was primarily intended for persons with back problems, many of whom wanted a portable solution. This is one of the reasons why this actual chair does not tilt but remains steady on the floor.

Since the chair is adjusted to have a steep seating angle, patients recovering from back surgery can begin to sit on a Multi chair, almost immediately after surgery. This posture is almost as easy on the back as a standing posture. The steep angle may put somewhat uncomfortable pressure on the shins, but if the posture reduces pain in the back, this disadvantage will be of secondary importance.

Multi is not intended to be a work chair but rather an all-round chair that has many advantages. It requires little space, is easy to fold up and easy to carry. It can also be hung on the wall.

A steeply angled seat will provide a favourable posture for the back while putting more pressure on the shins, whereas a flatter angled seat provides a poorer posture for the back but less pressure on the shins.

Multi balans®, STOKKE, 1981–2006 and VARIÉR, 2006–

Providing support where it is needed

A system for providing support for different parts of the body, for work while standing. The various support units that one might need can be plugged into a base as required. And they are all adjustable to the desired height.

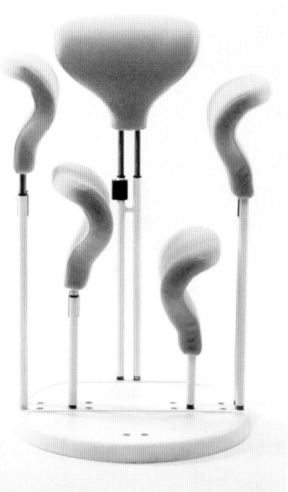

*balans® Supporter,
Studio HÅG, 1983*

balans® Supporter, 1982, prototype

On the borderline between sitting and standing

The word "sitting" is a general denotation for a range of bodily postures between standing upright and lying down. In the following pages, I will demonstrate various ways in which the human body can be supported. Many of these body postures are on the borderline between sitting and standing.

These and other unconventional supportive constructions for the human body were exhibited in the 1980s at the Scandinavian Furniture fair in Copenhagen, under the names "Westnofa Workshop" or "Studio HÅG".

balans® Femini/Maskuli, STOKKE, 1983, prototypes

Try to guess which is the Femini and which is the Maskuli

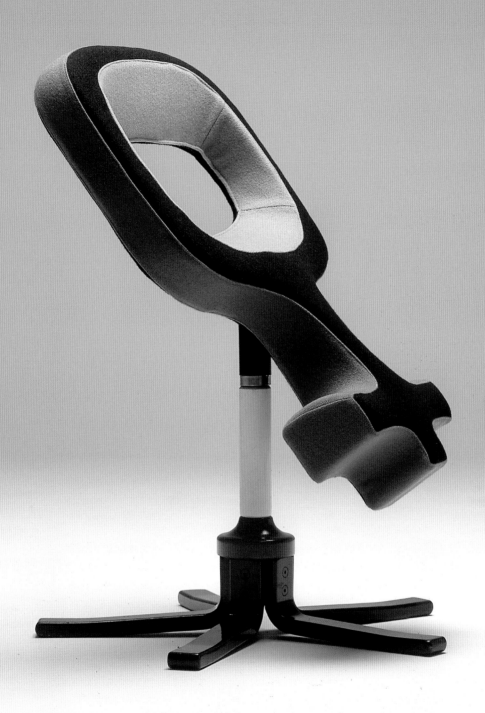

balans® Femini, STOKKE, limited edition, 1985-1989

Relax while standing

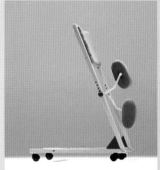

If we stand upright, leaning against a wall, and we then fall asleep in this position, why do we have a tendency to fall? The answer lies in the fact that we bend at the knees. The idea behind these standing supports was that they would counteract bending at the knees, allowing us to stand upright but at the same time with relaxed leg muscles. The soft cushion may be used optionally as support above or beneath the knee.

At the exhibition "Studio HÅG" in Copenhagen in 1983, we wandered around wearing tails

Is it merely the "backside" of the body that needs support?

It is often fascinating to sit on a staircase or on the rungs of a ladder. The sketches show experimentation with open supporting stands that provide comfortable bodily support even for the front of the body.

The relationship between the supporting elements and the openings between them is such that one can enjoy support on all sides of the body: front, back and lateral.

Sketches from 1982

126

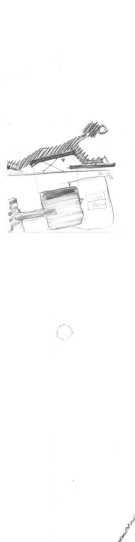

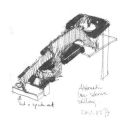

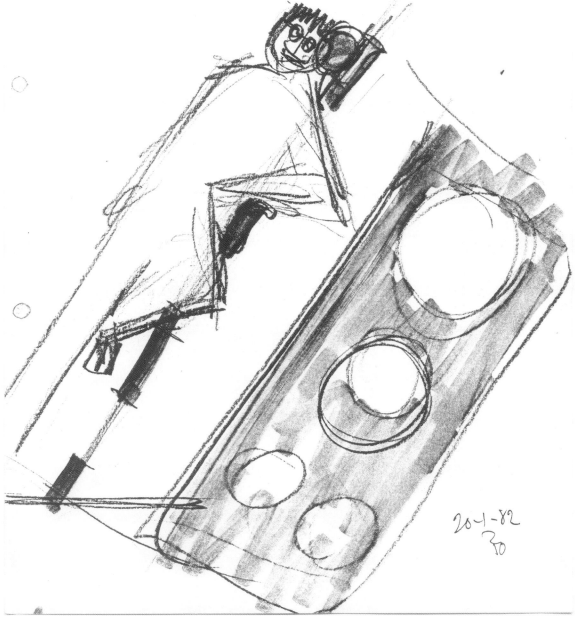

20-1-82
30

Can freedom be as important as support?

In this concept the seat and backrest have cut-out spaces for arms and legs, which gives the user freedom to vary his or her posture.

To facilitate many sitting postures, it is an advantage that the chair can be used with practically any of the table heights offered by modern adjustable desks.

Alternating between sitting high and sitting low during the workday provides welcome variation. When leaning forwards, we feel most comfortable sitting fairly high up, but when leaning back, it is nice to sit low and put one's feet up. When leaning forwards we get no support from a backrest, so why not sit on the chair backwards using the back support as a chest support?

The same variation can be achieved at a constant desk and seat height, if "HÅG StepUp" is attached. See page 133.

The inspiration for HÅG Capisco, "The Saddle Chair" was a horseback rider's dynamic posture. The goal, however, was to create a sitting device or work chair that would invite the user to assume the greatest number of sitting postures possible.

With HÅG Capisco the user can choose any thigh angle from almost vertical to horizontal.

Trying out the first and second prototype

The rider's bearing is natural compared with that afforded by a traditional chair. This inspired "The Saddle Chair".

HÅG Capisco, HÅG, 1984–

When the various experts on ergonomics were all promoting their one and only "correct" sitting posture, my comment was that all of them were right.

All of the recommended sitting postures were good, and I saw it as my job to design chairs that allowed as many different sitting postures as possible and to make it easier to move and change frequently between them.

Taking the "desires" of your feet seriously

Many of my work chairs are modular systems that support plug-in support devices for the various body parts: for the arms, head, legs, feet, etc. This provides a working space with greater possibilities to customize solutions for various work tasks without having to purchase many types of special chairs.

Adapter units that are attached to the central column may be rotated 180 degrees. For example, if one has a lot of work in a forward leaning posture, one can swing the leg support forward and assume a kneeling posture in order to alleviate stress on the lumbar region. If one wants to lean back to read documents, one can use the leg support as a footrest, and if one wants to remove it, the footrest may be rotated to the rear of the chair, or it can be detached entirely.

balans® Adapter units, 1985, various prototypes

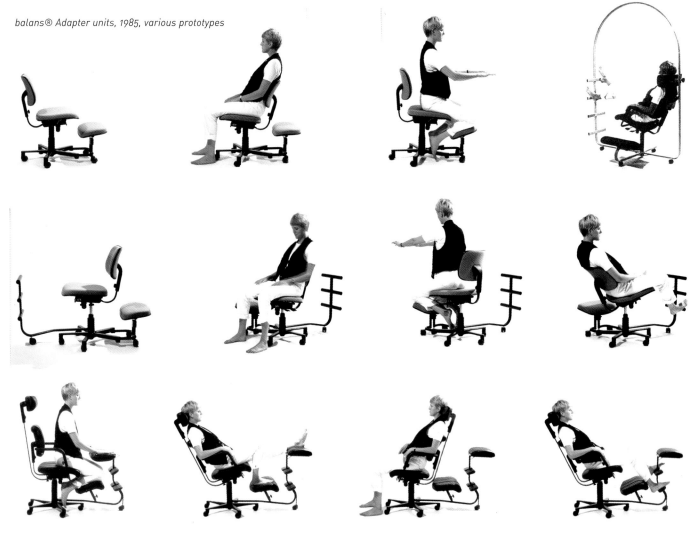

We all feel discomfort when we have to sit for a long time in the same position, and we often have the urge to move and change the position of our feet more frequently than our other body parts. If we sit for a while with our feet planted on the floor, we will soon seek an alternative place of support. If we do not find a suitable physical object nearby to put our feet on, we will often cross our legs for variety. See pages 44–55.

If we adjust the height of our office chairs so that we can work comfortably on something in front of us or leaning over our desks, what happens when we lean back to relax? That's right: we would like to have some sort of support for our feet in front of us and at a higher level. See page 47. StepUp makes this possible. It can easily swing out of the way when not needed and can be simply attached to or detached from the chair.

There is no single ideal place or ideal height for placing our feet when we sit. What we like is to have lots of options.

HÅG StepUp, HÅG, 1993 –

Feet "on" the table

To make even more sitting postures possible, it seemed natural to me to add extra support elements to the table legs.

If our feet are free to tilt us when we are seated, they will do so.

Centro, STOKKE, 1995–2000

A strap stretched between the legs of the table, or secured under the table top makes a simple – and welcome – foot support.

"Floors" of different heights

Since static working postures are a chief cause of musculoskeletal ailments, a working day should consist of as much versatility, movement and variation as possible.

One form of variation is alternating between standing and sedentary work. Height-adjustable desks (electric, hydraulic or with a crank) are the most common tools for achieving such variation. However, experience shows that the use of such height-adjustable desks rarely results in frequent alternation between a sitting and standing posture. One reason may be that adjusting the desk height requires a conscious act, i.e. personal initiative.

The sit/stand concept I describe here is based on having variation come naturally as a result of the body's wishes and from the work routines without the user needing to adjust desk or chair height.

This is possible by keeping the desk height the same all day long, whereas what is perceived as "the floor" has more than one height.

Why "floors" of different heights?

When we lean back in a chair, we often seek support for our feet far out in front of us and high up. However, when we sit hunched over our desks in an active work posture, we often pull our feet in under the seat. For this we would be more comfortable with the floor at a lower level.

Placing the desktop at a height for standing work makes it possible to build "floors" at these different levels. Whether in a forward-leaning or backward-leaning posture, with this concept, the user will automatically move his feet alternately between the different support levels while working.

This concept is most suitable where a high desk height is desirable because clients facing you on the other side are normally standing, such as in banks, post offices, travel agencies etc. In such situations, there should be no problem building floors or footrests of different heights without incurring major extra expenses.

See pages 44–55.

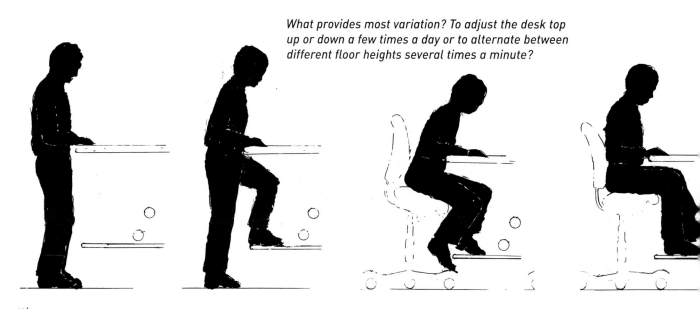

What provides most variation? To adjust the desk top up or down a few times a day or to alternate between different floor heights several times a minute?

Footrest as separate unit on the floor

Swivelling footrests mounted on the chair

Footrests mounted on the desk and on the chair

*First and second row: Sit/stand concept, 1990, prototypes
Third row: Sit/stand concept, 1990, used in a public office since 1993*

Our ancestors lived in the trees

We have become a sedentary society with a rather limited view of how we should fold our limbs when sitting. That is why, from the beginning of the 1980s, it was essential to demolish the stereotypical ideal of the proper sitting posture. To get this message across, I created a number of products or objects whose attention-getting impact was more important than their utility. Their purpose was to gain acceptance for a freer use of the body. *Garden* was developed more as a message than as a piece of furniture.

It is primarily intended for public spaces: one example is at airport meeting points, since the person who is waiting can see over the crowd and is also easily seen.

Trying out the first and second prototype, 1984

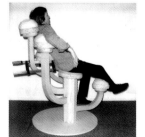

Should we take more heed of what our bodies tell us and be less concerned with conventions.

*Garden, STOKKE
1985–2005*

From the exhibition "T(h)ree Dimensions – Sculpture or Furniture", Oslo Museum of Applied Art, 1986

141

Wilderness

Go ahead, jump in and find a nest for your body.

From the exhibition "Primaerpunkt", Helsinki, 1989

Is a sofa merely for reclining?

I believe it is possible to make a sofa into a practical all-round sitting device.

The seat height of a sofa can be made relatively high if users, when reclining, have access to footrests under the table.

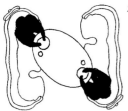

Sofa, 1990

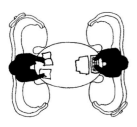

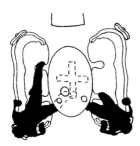

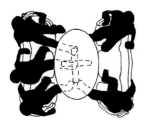

Notches in the seat for the legs permit users to sit in many directions. This may be useful when the TV is placed at one end of the sofa. This seat concept was designed in collaboration with my colleague Terje Ekstrøm.

Sofa, 1990

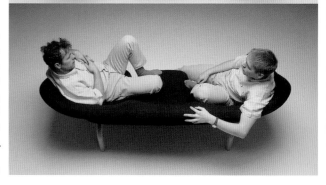

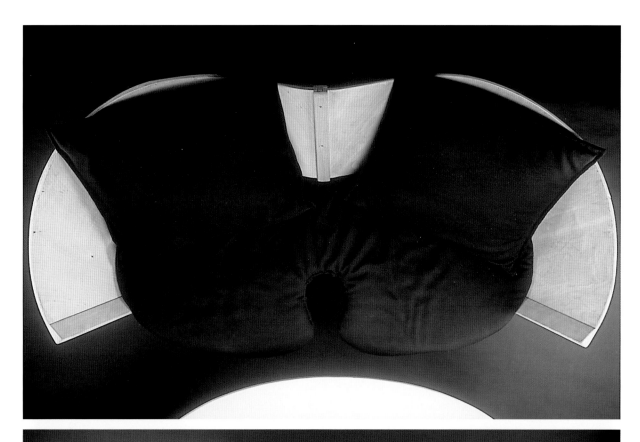

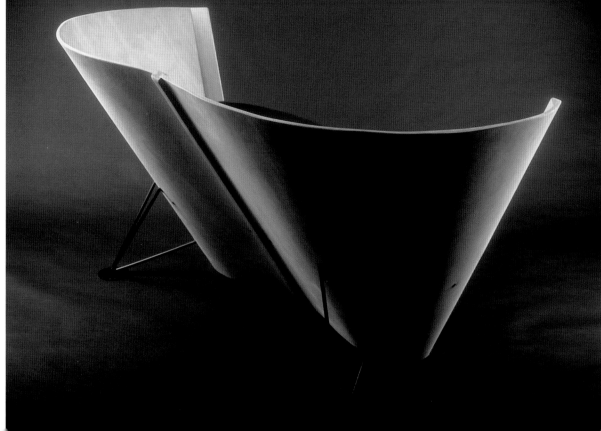

Alternative sofa

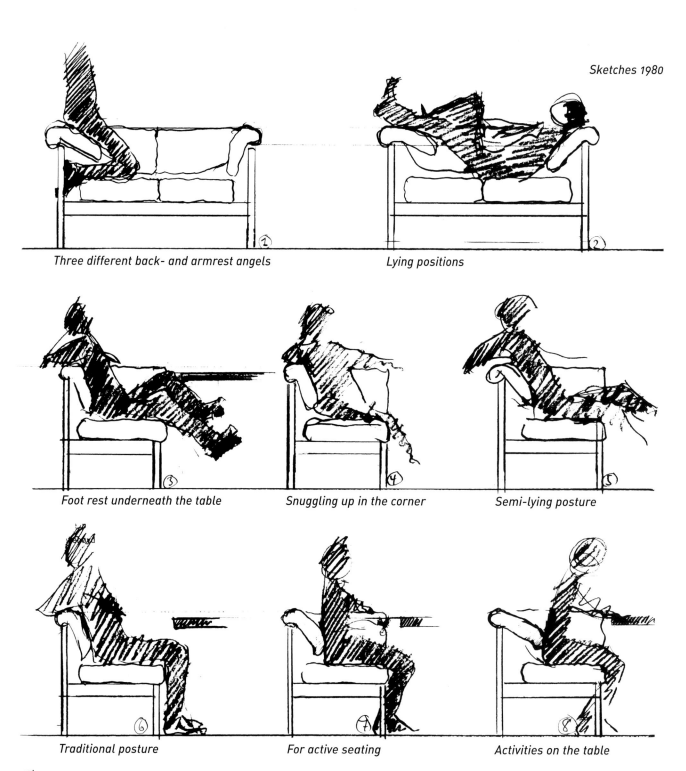

Sketches 1980

Three different back- and armrest angels

Lying positions

Foot rest underneath the table

Snuggling up in the corner

Semi-lying posture

Traditional posture

For active seating

Activities on the table

Stressful working postures

My suggestions for some professional groups
that have to work in stressful postures.

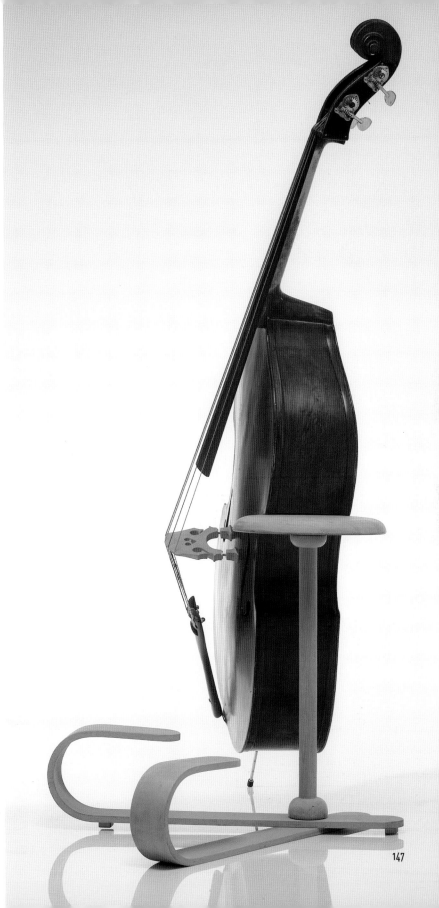

*Stool with footrests for
bass players, 1988*

Craftseat for people whose jobs require them to work on the ground or on the floor and a shin support for hairdressers.

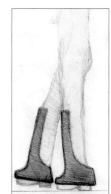 

The chair or shoe has a soft part for the shin, and a seat to sit on.

balans® Craftseat, 1985

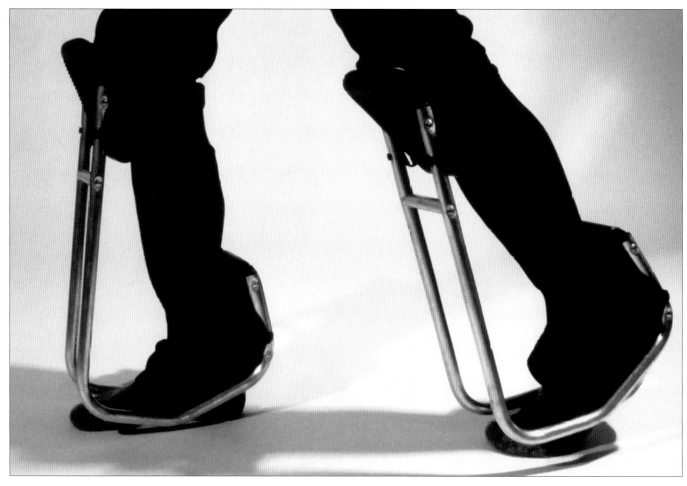

Taking your chair along may be practical because it will always be there when you need a place to sit.

Shin support, 1986, prototype

Sitting while being transported

We spend more and more time sitting down in various kinds of vehicles. Most of the topics on sitting in this book may naturally also apply to different modes of transport, including both the drivers and the passengers. I recommend the chapter "Favorite Postures" as a checklist when developing seating used in transportation.

Trainseat

The photos shows a suggestion from 1988 for seating for intermediate range trains, but the concepts underlying them should be applicable to buses and aeroplanes as well. The footrests and openings for the shoulders and elbows in these models provide freedom to sit alternatively.

Aboard aircraft I always think how wonderful it would be to have other points of support or surfaces to press your feet against higher up than the usual

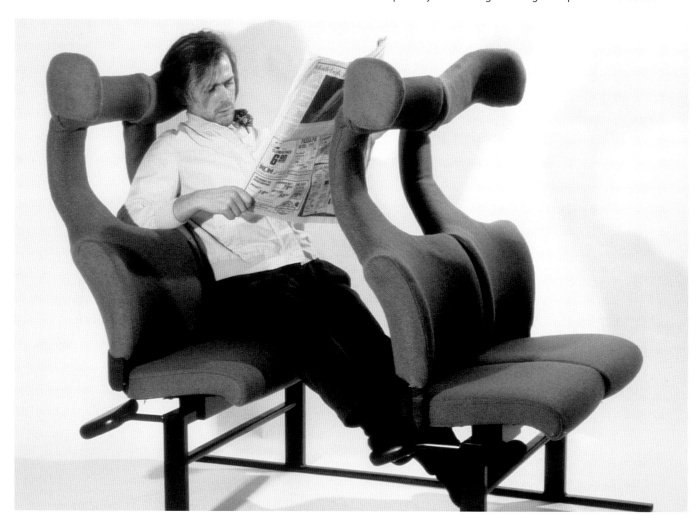

footrests. For example, why not behind the armrest on the row of seats in front of you?

I also wish that aeroplanes had seating that would allow good curvature of the back. An appropriate shape for backrests would also give fellow passengers in the seats behind you more room for their knees. The banana shaped backrests that are normally used for most aeroplane seating fail to support the lumbar region, and they reduce the knee room for the person sitting behind you.

The bus seats that have the best back curvature are often the narrowest city buses, probably not because the designers have placed more emphasis on ergonomics, but rather because of the lack of space available. In order to make room for as many passengers as possible, the backrest goes up vertically past the knees of the passenger in the seat behind before it begins to sweep backwards.

Train seats, 1988

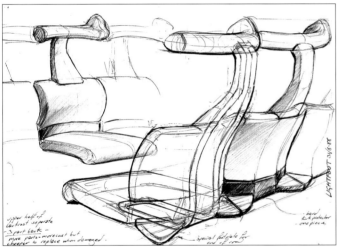

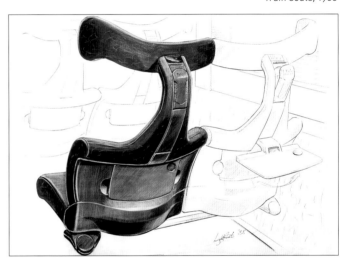

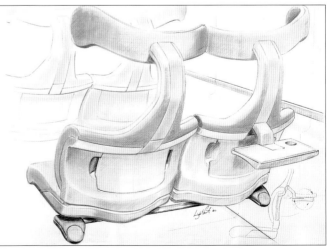

Dynamic automotive seating

In my view, all automotive seatings look exactly the same. It is bulky, static, and it lacks something as elementary as lumbar support.

I asked myself why the theories on dynamic sitting shouldn't also apply in cars and other modes of transport? According to the theory in "The chairs we 'wear'" on page 40, it must be considered unnatural to build a static structure around the human body, particularly in a mobile shell such as a vehicle.

Tilting pivoting backrest
In most cars we are seated too low down to be able to get any relief from the tilting principle that has been discussed earlier in this book. However, sitting in a car does have another advantage that can be exploited in a positive way. We have the opportunity to press or push our feet against the interior components directly in front of us without the seat sliding backwards. With the backrest tilting around the pivot, this possibility can be used to induce movement and to control the angle of a tilt-able backrest without the aid of a handle or lever.

Tilting pivoting seat front
The same tilting principle is used in the front part of the seat as in the backrest. This gives the option of elevating the front of the seat for appropriate support for the thighs.

When entering and exiting a vehicle, the front of the seat is low. The front edge of the seat rises when the weight of the user's body presses the rear part of the tilting surface down. See page 113. Supports for the thighs are flexible and independent of each other, to allow for convenient operation of the clutch pedal.

Liberating/supporting the right foot
In what part of the body does one become tired first when driving a car? The answer of course is in the muscles of the right leg. This is because the right leg is exposed to static stress from maintaining steady pressure on the accelorator pedal.

Solutions:
- Optional foot support near the foot-controlled accelerator to avoid static strain. The accelerator can be controlled by twisting the foot.
- An additional, simple hand-controlled accelerator, as found in cars from the 1930s.
- An additional, manually operated accelerator device placed on the wheel, as on motorcycles.
- Cruise control, as found in the more expensive car models today.

Manually operated devices would remove the need for continual static pressure on the accelerator. In addition, this would allow drivers to be able to stretch out and move their legs from time to time while using the hand-controlled accelerator. The above mentioned solutions, in my opinion, should have been given priority over automatic gears and electric windows.

In this project I am asking if dynamic seating will lead to a better working environment for drivers, and also whether it will make the driver more alert, thereby leading to improved safety?

Have you ever tried jumping on the ground after jumping on a trampoline? I have the same feeling when I sit in a static, conventional automotive seat after driving with the dynamic solution presented here.

The slim backrest gives 10–20 cm extra knee room for back-seat passengers.

Another logic solution is letting the active driver sit elevated and upright, while the passengers are reclining sitting at a lower level.

Optional foot support for back-seat passengers.

chapter 6
size

When ergonomics was introduced as a tool in the development of sitting furniture, it was the product's physical suitability to the human body that was focused upon first and foremost. If consumers are to profit from the primary principles expounded in this bookthe products should have physical measurements that are suitable to the consumer's physique. A three-year-old is only about half the height of an adult and there is a considerable challenge in wanting these two disparate individuals to use the same piece of furniture for sitting.

Mini Max

The purpose of this chair was to create an adjustable seating solution for ages ranging from 6–7 years to adult. The chair's form and design are intended to make it easy to adjust the functional dimensions to the user's size.

The side members are bent at such an angle that the seating depth automatically increases as the seat/backrest is moved upwards.

If you place the seat, backrest and tabletop in hole 3, the following dimensions are supposed to be in the proper reciprocal relationship:
* The seat height above the floor.
* The seat depth back to the backrest.
* The height of the backrest above the seat.
* The difference between seat height and tabletop height.

Mini Max, STOKKE, 1970–1975

Growing with the child

The classic "high chairs" can be used by babies up until they reach the age of about two years. In 1972 the only sitting devices for children from the age of two and upwards were special, low chairs, where the child sat with his feet on the floor.

When the children sat at the adult's table, they used ordinary chairs designed and intended for grown-ups.

My objective was that one chair should seat persons of all sizes from approximately 8 months and up, in a natural way at the same table. The concept should provide normal, functional dimensions for children of different sizes as well as adults. My hope was that this would make sitting at the table more enjoyable and make it easier to perform activities there. By having small children sit on a higher seat than adults, the height difference is reduced, improving interaction between children and adults. Mealtimes may become more relaxed, and children find it easier to concentrate on the activities taking place around the table when the physical environment has been adapted to their size and needs.

I started by drawing all sizes of people with their elbows at tabletop level. Since the elbows and lower back are at the same level, the chair's backrest could be permanently fixed at tabletop height. The only parts that had to be adjustable were the seat and the

I looked around for a chair that allowed my two-year-old son to sit in a natural way at the grown-ups' table. I had to figure out the solution myself. Here he is, four years later, still happy.

Tripp Trapp, STOKKE, 1972–

footrest. These had to be adjustable with regard to both height and depth. As noted earlier in the book, it is the feet that control most of our movements, including when we are seated. This is why it is important to have a broad and solid foot support adjusted at the correct height. This "floor" provides the child with control over his own body movements and it facilitates movement and a continuous change of sitting posture.

The classic type of "high chair" had no footrest or merely a rod or small shelf upon which the child could put her feet. In most cases, the child's feet didn't even reach the footrest, and when they did reach it, the footrest was so narrow that it limited the feet to a fixed placement.

The newer type of "high chairs" that are sold in a number of countries are often the recliner type because they are used already in the infant's first months, often as a chair suitable for feeding the baby. When the child is given this kind of recliner chair, it will often be used for a long time beyond the point at which the child is able and wants to sit actively with a vertically balanced upper torso.

To be forced to lie in a chair when one wants to sit actively and balanced in an upright position is an unfortunate situation for the child. Most of

Double-size furniture is a way of understanding how three-year-olds perceive their surroundings.

these chairs have a reclining seat which is not an ideal platform for sitting upright. The baby also has difficulties bending or pulling her legs up under the seat because of the partition or cushion between the seat and the footrest.

I also wonder why some countries have a safety harness requirement, which results in the two-year-olds being strapped into the chair. In my models, they usually climb in and out of the chair at will before that age. Why shouldn't children of that age be able to climb up and down from the chair when they want to? I think the safety harness requirements in these countries exist because their children's chairs are not designed to give the child this freedom When a two-year-old has to climb in and out of this type of chair it is unsafe, since the child has to climb over the tray.

Try changing your position while sitting with your legs dangling unsupported.

"Classified advert: Long life"

I am delighted that Tripp Trapp is always listed under the "Wanted" column in the classified ads and is hardly ever found in the "For sale" column. I take this as a sign that it is a product that enjoys a long service life. The design of the chair has not been changed since 1973. This means that a child that inherits its Tripp Trapp chair from its parents does not feel different from a child that has a brand new one.

It is said that the greatest competition facing Tripp Trapp in Scandinavia is second-hand Tripp Trapp-chairs that are inherited or sold to new generations of families with small children.

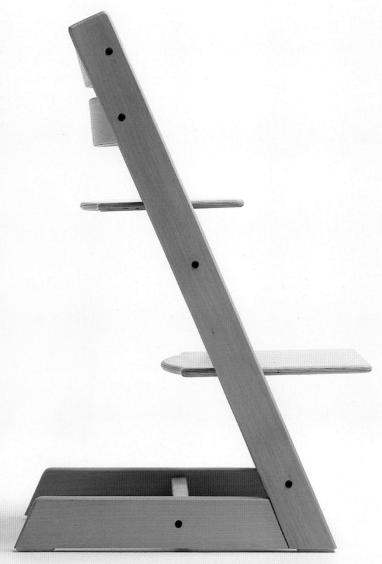

Generation chair: The chair that grows with the child from infancy to adulthood.

The sandbag
and the rubber ball

I've often been asked why my chairs for children are static (not tilting), when movement, tilting or rocking is so important in the chairs I design for adults. There are many reasons for this difference. For infants and toddlers, safety is essential, of course, and this can hardly be associated with chairs that rock and tilt. To be acceptable, a chair for infants and toddlers must meet the standards and regulations that the various countries have for such chairs.

Even if the aforementioned regulations did not exist, making a static chair for infants, toddlers and small children would probably still be the right thing to do. Have you ever heard of children who need encouragement to move around?

If we make a comparison in which adults in the industrialized world are sandbags and young children are rubber balls, we might then ask ourselves which support surface is best for creating movement and variation in position for the one group as opposed to the other. Adults need something to get them moving and something to facilitate that movement. For this reason most of my chairs for adults are equipped with features that allow easy, gentle movements. Children, however, bounce around and thus need a solid base that enables them to move in the way they do. This is why Tripp Trapp stands solidly on the floor and has a sturdy seat and a spacious footrest that provides support for the child's active movement.

Kids need no encouragement to move around.

*Tripp Trapp,
STOKKE, 1972–*

162

The Norwegian architectural journal Byggekunst called Tripp Trapp "the chair that transformed day-care centres". Day-care centres, nursery schools and kindergartens used to be furnished with low tables and small chairs. In Scandinavia, most such institutions now have areas with regular "grown-up" tables and Tripp Trapp-chairs. This improved the relationship between teachers and children of different sizes. An added benefit is that teachers do not have to bend down to the level of low tables all the time.

It is important for small children to be able to spend as much time as possible on the floor or on flat surfaces, where they have full freedom to develop motor control.

On a Tripp Trapp chair, smaller children sit on a higher seat than the taller ones, and this lessening of height differences improves interaction between children and grown-ups.

Easy to climb, easy to adjust

Since the existing product (Tripp Trapp) functioned superbly, the question is: why develop a new product just like it? The answer is that Sitti is not "just like it". It satisfies the same fundamental needs as the Tripp Trapp, but as the pictures show, it does this in a quite different manner. Those for whom the following points are relevant can choose this chair:

1. In an environment where visiting toddlers often put in an appearance, the ability to adjust the chair quickly without needing tools is definitely an advantage.

2. Because of its open form, the chair is easier for the child to get in and out of without having to be moved to and from the table.

3. The chair has a playful, sculptural shape.

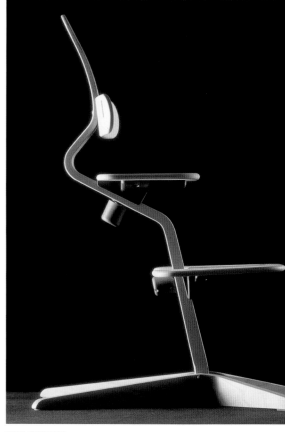

Sitti, STOKKE, 1993–

"Adjust to your own measurements in 10 seconds"

History

In 1977 I developed the concept from which Stokke made pilot series for furnishing a classroom. The furniture was in daily use until 2005. In 1998 the concept was redesigned, and I show both designs here.

Product advantages

Organization
- One is able to purchase a single type and size for the entire school.
- Pupils can move and be moved within and between classrooms and are always able to enjoy chairs and desks with suitable dimensions.
- All desktops have the same height, making them suitable for grouping.
- All classrooms are at the same time well-suited to adult education, parent–teacher conferences, etc.

Schooldesk, STOKKE, 1977–1978

Ergonomics
- Only two elements, the seat and foot-board, are moved to ensure that these four dimensions are correct:
  - The difference between seat height and desktop height
  - Seat height above the "floor"
  - Seat depth
  - The height of the backrest above the seat.

- Each pupil learns his own seat and footboard code, e.g. C4 or E7.

- The same station can be adapted for pupils from primary through lower secondary school.

- More accurate adjustments can be made than on desks with fixed dimensions.

- More than one level for placing the feet facilitates variations between sitting postures.

- Smaller children sit on a higher seat than taller ones, which has a beneficial psychological and communicative impact.

- The teacher does not have to bend as much when helping a pupil at his or her desk.

Schooldesk, 1998, redesign

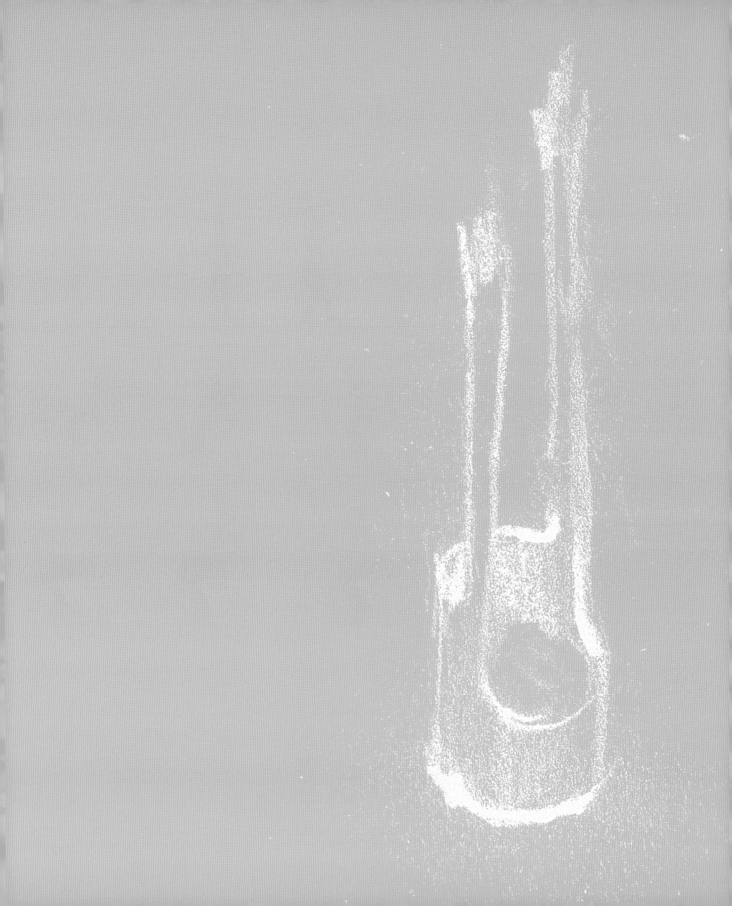

rethinking sitting

chapter 7
other qualities than the ergonomic

Imagine that you are a buyer who must purchase furniture for the lobby of an institution or company. The room needs two types of sitting furniture. One type is furniture for those who work seven hours a day behind the desk in the lobby.

The other type is to be used in the lounge portion of the lobby by visitors who may have to wait a few minutes before being received for their appointments.

When the furniture for these two areas of use is considered, the different needs or criteria for each should be evaluated separately. For the work chairs, ergonomics and function should be the most important factors. For the furniture in the lounge group, however, visual form in harmony with the architecture and profile of the institution should be given highest consideration.

The examples in this chapter may tend to be the antithesis of the products in chapters 4, 5 and 6. In order to make the point that ergonomics does not always have to be the most important criterion for sitting furniture, I will demonstrate here a number of examples of my own works where visual form, expression, flexibility or the environment are more important.

Cubistic forms

In many instances where the chairs will be utilized for only a short period of time, the item can be expressive rather than having ergonomic qualities.

Sculpture or furniture?

Functionality?

I have used the chair Embracement in the hall of my apartment. Its functionality as a piece of sitting furniture is not at all important in this area of use, but it is pleasant that the chair "embraces" me when I sit down for a few seconds to take off my shoes. In the same manner, it is pleasing when the Hands chair, located in this same space, pulls at its hair and stretches out its arms in happiness over seeing me, offering me one of its fingers on which to hang my jacket.

Environment

We tend not to get rid of things that are unusual, untraditional and unique as easily as we do run-of-the-mill objects. The objects in the Cylindra series are out of the ordinary, sophisticated and made of natural materials. I hope that in the future, they will be among the objects that are sought after as antiques from our era.

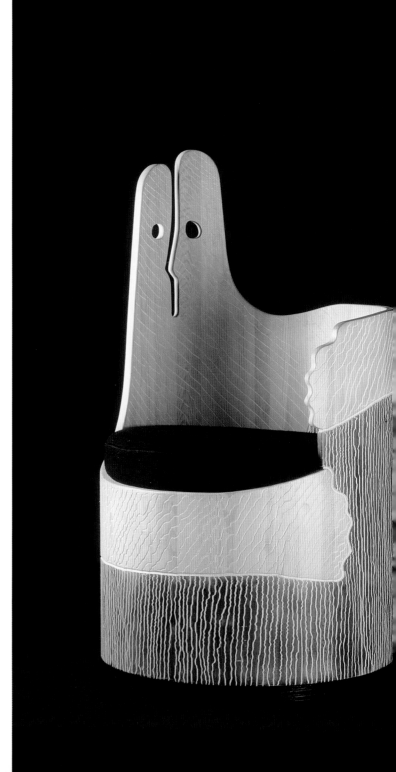

Embracement, CYLINDRA, 1986–

172

Hands, CYLINDRA, 1986–

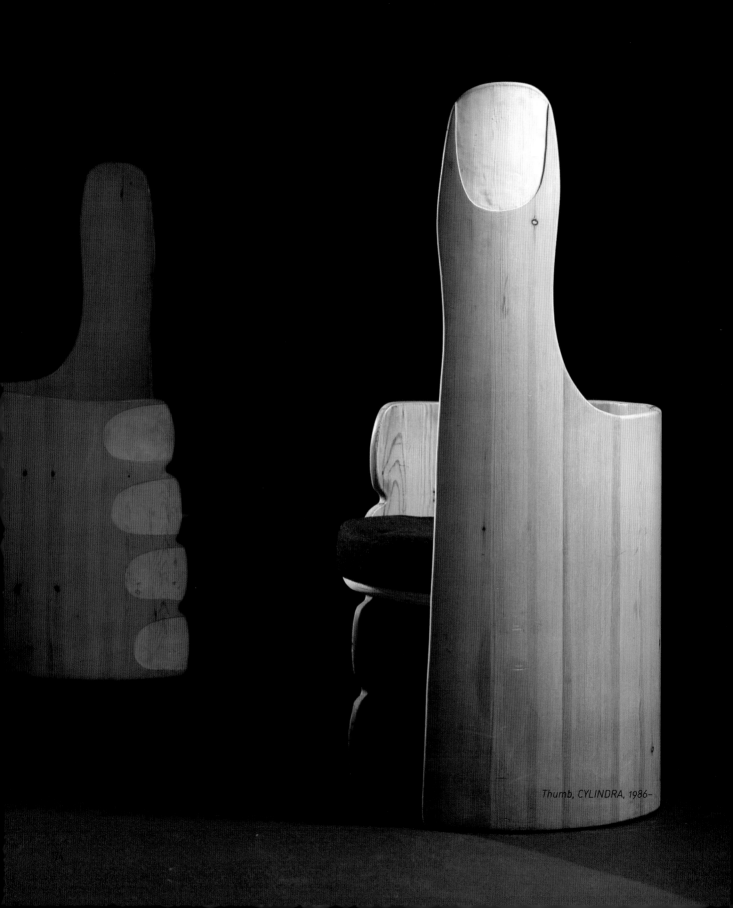

Thumb, CYLINDRA, 1986–

Chair with hair, CYLINDRA, 1986

Transformable objects

Here I present examples of furniture products where the need for flexibility, visual impact and environmental aspects are more important than having a good seat to sit on.

Flexibility

Nowadays, large numbers of the population change residences far more often than was common previously, especially in large cities. In addition, over half of the households in our major cities consist of singles, and many of them do not have large living spaces.

The objects can be hung on the wall or placed against the wall standing on their own legs. When you're entertaining guests and need more seats and tables, this furniture can easily be assembled. Just move the arms and legs around and these sculptures become instant furniture.

Most of the furniture in ordinary furniture shops still looks as if it is meant for nuclear families with their own home and a large number of rooms. The lack of suitable furniture products for the emerging urban nomads was the reason that I developed these furniture systems.

Expression

Many households suffer from a lack of storage space, especially for large items like furniture. When Nomadi is "in storage", the owner can be proud of having this storage visible in the room. Furniture that is not in use can be transformed into sculptures by placing the legs on the side of the sculpture to create a completely new expression.

Environment

Ten reasons why Nomadi is less harmful to the environment than most furniture:

1. Space. It takes up little space when being transported or stored, which in turn gives the users fewer reasons to get rid of it.
2. Timelessness. It is not trendy, so it won't quickly go out of fashion.
3. Service life. With the love that went into the crafting, it is more likely to have a long service life.
4. Functionality. We more readily get rid of less useful items than things that really help us.
5. Oddity. We more readily get rid of generic items than things that are special and peculiar.
6. Flexibility. Things with several different applications may be well worth keeping.
7. Material. Wood is a renewable resource.
8. Material consumption. The plywood veneer has been lathe-peeled from the log and this means a high degree of utilisation and little waste.
9. Weight. It is a lightweight design.
10. Assembly. It is assembled without metal parts, screws or special tools.

"Family on the wall" from the Nomadi concept, displayed at the Röhss Museum for Applied Art and Design in Gothenburg, 2000

Nomadi, 2001
Left side sculptures, right side furniture

When Nomadi is "in storage" the owner can be proud of having this storage visible in the room. The objects can be hung on the wall or placed against the wall standing on their own legs.

When you're entertaining guests and need more seats and tables, this furniture can be assembled in the blink of an eye. Just move the arms and legs around and these sculptures become furniture.

Nomadi, displayed at the Oslo Museum of Applied Art, 2000

Four kilos of comfort

A lightweight chair built for flexibility on the same principles as the Nomadi: an attempt to achieve as much comfort as possible using as few resources as possible.

A simple knock-down construction with no metal parts that occupies a minimum of space in storage.

A chair designed for everyone in general and for the emerging urban nomads in particular.

Safari, NATURELLEMENT, 2002–2006

A symbol of movement

This chair is more a symbol of movement
and flexibility than it is an incarnation of
these criteria. A coil spring is a symbol
of softness and resilience. For a contest
in 1975, I attempted to create a chair
that was wound from a long steel tube,
a small model of which was designed
and built. Some years later I suggested
a technique for manufacturing this chair,
and 50 copies were made.

Python, CYLINDRA, 1990–2000

rethinking sitting

chapter 8
observations and inspirations

I have already attempted to demonstrate how criteria dictated by the human body have been decisive in the development of most of my sitting devices. Indeed, this is the main topic of this book, but I would also like to look at some of the other aspects of my field that I find interesting, such as the creative process and various social and ecological issues. The titles of the sections in this chapter are self-explanatory. Some of the ideas expressed may not seem to fit in with the rest of the book. Nevertheless, I have chosen to include them.

In many cases, the same type of sitting furniture will function well in a number of different areas. A work chair, for example, can equally well be used at the dining table. In other cases, however, areas of use may entail completely different criteria. Let us now imagine two separate situations, each requiring us to sit for a period of three hours. In the first situation, we are stuck at the airport because of a delayed flight. We are sitting in the waiting area in a relatively fancy chair. In the second situation, we are sitting in a café in the company of good friends, and we are seated on small, hard chairs. Most frequent flyers have probably experienced being stuck in the airport lounge and becoming very uncomfortable, whereas few of us have distasteful memories of having used non-functional chairs in restaurants.

This brings us to theories on how the mind affects our experience of our physical surroundings. No one enjoys having to wait for a delayed flight – it's boring and it doesn't take long before you are painfully aware of the top of the chair back digging into your shoulders as you try to relax in a more reclined posture. By contrast, when we are out with friends, we are often having such a good time that we scarcely notice what we are sitting on. We can therefore infer the general rule from these observations that our experience of a situation is often of greater significance for how we react to our physical surroundings than is the design of the surroundings per se.

Is it correct to say, then, that we should choose comfortable sitting furniture only in places where we will most likely become bored? Obviously not. The persons who are responsible for choosing furniture for their own use or for others should carefully consider the situations in which the ergonomic qualities discussed in this book are important, and the situations in which they are less important. The governing rule should be that our surroundings must be as well adapted to our human needs as possible. This does not always have to be equated with cost, but the planning and design of furniture require knowledge and careful consideration.

The living room

Historical background

In former times, most people worked in immediate or close proximity to their residences.

The residence itself was frequently also one's workplace. If we look far enough back in time, we find that domestic activities were carried out around the fireplace, a place of warmth and light. These activities would have included handicrafts, needlework, repairs, food preparation, etc. Later on, long tables and benches came into use in our western part of the world, and life around the long table was perhaps an active one. When a person wanted to relax or rest, this could be done on benches or beds.

During the Renaissance, the middle classes introduced chairs as living room furnishings. Kitchens became a communal part of the house and absorbed some of the activities that had previously been carried out in the living room. However, in farmhouses and in workers' homes, the living room was still ascribed functions other than as a place to relax. The middle classes now had several rooms, thereby allowing one or more of the best living rooms to be reserved for receiving guests and for special occasions. These specially reserved parlours became the models for our modern day lounges or living rooms.

The Industrial Revolution had an impact on living arrangements, particularly on living rooms and furnishings. When gainful employment was moved out of the living quarters, this naturally resulted in rendering the household living room passive.

My question is whether the manner in which modern living rooms in our part of the world are furnished is truly conducive to the activities that people want to carry out there.

If the earlier farmhouse living room had served as a model, the living rooms of our modern era would more likely be a place for all kinds of activities, such as repairing outboard motors, working at looms and woodworking benches, working at the computer, etc.

Analysis

A simple table showing the activities we carry out while sitting in our living rooms may help us to understand the range of our furniture needs:

Passive ←————————————————→ *Active*				
	Listening to music	Conversing	Eating	Writing, using a laptop
Sleeping	Watching television	Talking on the telephone	Drinking	Playing games, chess, cards
Snoozing dreaming	Reading	Reading	Dinner parties	Needle-work
Dozing				Homework

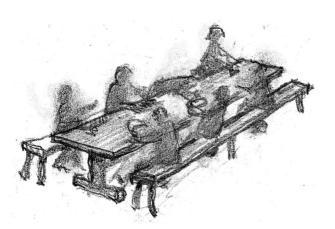

It appears to me that our modern, western living rooms cater for the examples on the left-hand side of the table more readily than for those on the right-hand side. In our part of the world, the relaxation side of the spectrum is increasing at the expense of the physical space that would be most suitable for activities.

During the functionalist movement of the 1930s, new architects and designers started basing the design of interior décor and objects on the modern lifestyle of the era. Today, however, there is little debate about what type of home environment best fulfils our different needs.

In the illustration we see that most of the activities on the right-hand side (generally) require a table, while those on the left do not. This is only natural since we generally need a surface to support or store what we are working on. One would think that as fewer and fewer of us perform physically demanding work outside the home, we would have developed a better home environment for different types of activities, but this does not appear to be the case – with the notable exception of preparing food. Never before has cooking been so popular, and the kitchen is often the most finely furnished room in the home, precisely because this is where creative activities are performed.

All of us have experienced that the most memorable conversations and discussions frequently take place when we are seated around a high table, such as a dining table or conference table, rather than when we are lounging on sofas or in easy chairs.

Communal activities such as eating, playing cards, writing, drawing, building model aeroplanes, reading the newspaper, etc. are easier at high tables than when seated in low furniture designed for relaxation.

For the majority of the world's population, these thoughts are nothing more than an inconsequential luxury problem, but I am raising the issue here because this kind of analysis may represent a way for those of us living in industrialized countries to obtain improved quality of life in our living spaces.

The traditional middle-class approach to living arrangements is to have one area or room solely for relaxing, another for eating, another for working, another for sleeping, etc. This traditional compartmentalisation hardly represents an optimal use of available resources if the aim is to achieve the best possible quality of life per square metre. This implies that there are also ecological reasons for thinking differently and trying to achieve a higher level of comfort in less space.

Media/IT developments have also contributed to outdating the idea of compartmentalised living areas. Our increasing dependence on the TV screen has made it more and more common to have meals seated on the sofa rather than at the dining room table. Most types of work done at home no longer require a special work room in the residence; with laptops, our work can be done literally anywhere. With this in mind, it would not be disadvantageous if the various kinds of sitting furniture in our homes were compatible with both working and relaxing. The chair at the kitchen table and the chair in the traditional lounge area should both provide the possibility for beneficial work postures as well as comfortable relaxation.

In many of the large cities today, about half of the residential units are occupied by single persons, many of them in small flats. This is one reason why it is natural to begin thinking of furnishing living quarters in a new way.

At furniture trade fairs, I go wandering around for days on end looking at a seemingly infinite number of sofas and recliners designed, with all their softness and luxury, to make a sedentary lifestyle as comfortable as possible. There is almost always a superfluity of soft, comfortable elements that are intended to make one's use of such devices as comfortable as possible. The fact that they are so soft that they render the sitting quality miserable is another matter; the intention is to make the experience pleasant for us.

When chairs designed for sitting at eating/working height are exhibited, the comfort of the sitter seldom seems to have been taken into consideration. It is likely that our bodies will be forced to endure minimalist, static and hard "racks" or high-backed "chieftain's chairs" from which the only relief is the end of the one-hour meal when we can leave the table.

So what forces are at play that lead us to furnish our living rooms in such a non-functional manner? Or to put it slightly differently: do the distributors, manufacturers and designers of furniture have an identifiable philosophy concerning the way people should live? Even though most furniture products do indeed express normative thoughts about preferred lifestyles, I do not think that the majority of manufacturers and designers have an explicitly formulated philosophy on a conscious level.

In the 1980s, brochures from Norwegian sofa manufacturers showed tuxedo-clad people standing around, pretending that everyday life was one long cocktail party. Television series like *Upstairs Downstairs* and *Falcon Crest* set the standards for the day.

Maybe designers should start by asking a fundamental question: does the way we furnish our homes make them a good place for us to carry out the activities that we would like to carry out there?

The home office

The arrival of industrialization meant that gainful employment generally had to be done outside the home, and this remained the norm in industrialized countries for many generations. However, in today's post-industrial society, the home is again becoming a workplace. Researchers predicting how society will be in the future tell us that an increasing number of people are going to spend more and more time at home. Certain technological developments, not least of all those in the IT sector, make it easier for us to work from home. One argument in favour of increasing the amount of work done from home is our need to reduce the energy, space and time used transporting people to and from work.

If it is indeed true that we are currently in the middle of a dramatic change in our lifestyles, designers ought to seize the opportunity to ask themselves what furniture best suits these new social patterns.

As we enter an era with an increasing amount of sedentary work being done at home, we will be faced with a choice of improving home working conditions either by preparing a special workplace with suitable office furniture, or alternatively by furnishing our homes with chairs that are also suitable for work. You can probably guess what my choice would be. I believe we should try to furnish our homes with dynamic furniture for sitting that suits the combined demands of leisure, family activities and work. The body's natural needs remain the same, whether you are eating dinner or preparing a document for your next meeting.

In my opinion, you do not need to have special office furniture at home in order to have a home office. If most of the chairs in your home were designed for both forward and backward leaning postures, you would have the best conditions for all the traditional activities around the home (table?) and also for any professional work that is done there. This type of furniture would provide a high level of flexibility, as each part of your home that has a chair would also be a potential workplace. Several people could choose to participate in activities around one large table or, if a more isolated setting is preferred, each person could work in a separate room. The growing use of laptop computers further increases this flexibility.

The office in focus

Ergonomics has concentrated on the workplaces of some professions more than others – and for good reason. In many professions, tools were often designed first, and the person who was employed to use them had to adapt as best he could to the machine. For example, I know that crane operators have difficult working conditions, as do cashiers in supermarkets, automobile mechanics, etc.

With the increasing construction of office buildings as workplaces, offices have naturally become the focus for ergonomists, furniture manufacturers and designers – myself included. Paradoxically, all the attention has in fact resulted in a rather narrow view concerning which solutions are best. There are any number of standards for work chairs, containing highly detailed descriptions of their shape, size, dimensions and strength. For a designer, these standards serve to hinder and even prevent unconventional solutions from gaining popularity in the workplace. It is almost impossible to get these kinds of chairs approved in official regulations and standards.

As far as chairs are concerned, it has taken a very long time to gain acceptance for even relatively small alternative improvements. One example is gaining acceptance for the forward tilt of the seat pan.

For obvious reasons, it is easier for an individual to decide to buy an item for his or her personal use than it is for a purchasing department to choose what to buy for a large number of users. After almost 20 years, HÅG *Capisco*, "the saddle chair", has at long last been accepted in large companies too. My wooden chairs with curved runners are not found in many large offices and industrial premises, but are a popular choice among individual buyers. One of the reasons for this might be that all the standards for office chairs are based on one type of chair with a star base, central column, etc. Another reason might be that the industry has focused on the ability to adjust a chair to the size and height of the user as the most important functional criterion.

HÅG Capisco, HÅG, 1984–, Fabrics: Ellinor Flor

What is work?

How was your day, darling?
Ugh! Meetings all day, one after the other, I am utterly exhausted.

When is your body happiest – after a day of meetings, or after a day at your normal place of work? The answer, of course, depends on what your normal work is. But for many of us, the answer will be that our bodies are happiest on the days when we have been at our normal workplace. I would like to suggest three reasons for this:

- In a meeting, you probably have much *less space* in which to vary the posture of your body than you do in your normal workplace.
- In a meeting, you probably have to sit *for a longer period of time* than you would in your normal workplace.
- In meetings/conferences, *you have to be better behaved* than you do in your normal workplace where, for example, you may be able to put your feet up on the desk.

These three factors suggest that there is a greater need for dynamic chairs in meeting rooms and conference rooms than in the personal office.

In different professions, an increasing number of people are finding that a growing portion of their time is spent in meetings and conferences. This is a neglected area of concern, ergonomically speaking. Meetings can often follow in quick succession and may be poorly planned.

Most suppliers of office seating try to make life comfortable for you in your personal space at your own workplace, whereas the same concern has not even been addressed for meetings that may follow one another for days on end.

A few decades ago, high status was associated with sitting in meetings or attending conferences. Society showed great respect for these hallowed halls in which important decisions were made, and special types of chairs were developed for these rooms, for which the most important design factors were style and authority. The phenomenon "conference seating" is further proof of how the "authoritative sitting" of earlier historical times continues to influence the design of today's chairs.

In an attempt to address such challenges, we should take into account that our meeting chairs are also work chairs, and they should be designed with the same possibilities for tilting that have become standard on chairs for use in permanent workplaces. Another argument for providing more possibilities for movement in the seating is that offices of the future will probably be more flexible and will not require that everyone has an individual, personal workplace. Conference rooms and meeting tables equipped with this type of chair can then become adequate workplaces in themselves.

Dynamic conference

The working environment

In Norway – a country with a mere five million inhabitants – muscular and skeletal diseases cost society NOK 15 billion per year, according to the national daily paper, Aftenposten. It is an indisputable fact that long-term sitting is a major cause of many of our muscular and skeletal complaints, and it is this category of sitting that I feel it is important to rethink. Developing chairs or sitting devices that actually encourage more active sitting is a concrete response to a problem facing thousands and thousands of people.

I would also like to mention one more fundamental prerequisite for our day-to-day well-being: how we organize our work. It is essential that our everyday work is sufficiently varied to avoid static working postures and a static working situation in a more general context. Employees must be able to take part in decision-making and to influence their everyday situation. Furthermore, it is just as important that the tasks we perform seem meaningful, so that we feel that we are an important part of the process. Another element that is often underestimated is awareness of one's own body. Each and every person ought to be aware of the way in which the human body functions, so that they can enjoy using it in the way nature intended.

No shortage of materials!

Chairs in snow, 1965

How ideas come about

From my own experience, I suggest that ideas for new products arise somewhere between the following two poles:

1. A desire to solve a problem
2. A desire to express form

The products illustrated in chapters 3–6 were initiated out of a desire to solve a problem or to improve unsatisfactory solutions. Most of the products in chapter 7, on the other hand, were developed because I wanted to express myself artistically.

As far as industrial applied-art products are concerned, the usual course of events is normally that the designer conceives or is given a visual idea that he or she then refines further to a finished product. The functional elements are important, of course, but are often second in priority to visual appearance. With this kind of innovation, it is the need for expression – not the desire to solve a problem – that is the designer's primary creative driving force.

New materials, new manufacturing techniques or new principles of construction may also provide the impetus to begin development of innovative products. In terms of initiating developmental projects in the field of industrial design, the commission or assignment often comes from industrial management.

Throughout the history of mankind, solving problems has been a potent driving force. Indeed, the very development of society is a result of the fact that a number of keen souls have striven to find solutions to problems. Inventors want to solve problems, and inside every designer there is an inventor. For example, a very common approach to innovation is to take weaknesses in existing products as a point of departure and then look for ways to overcome them or find original new solutions.

One issue, then, is whether designers should try to meet the demands of the market or create products that are designed on the basis of our own assessment of what is important. For example, since the majority of people who are out to buy furniture choose with their eyes, not their bodies, should we simply follow their lead and offer visually pleasing and often less functional solutions, or should we offer correctives in the form of functional products?

For me personally, the most common working method has been to register a need (or a need for improvement) that I see as important and then try to develop a solution or a product that will meet this need.

In many cases, becoming aware of the need may be the most valuable moment. Finding the solution is often more of an analytical process.

The Tripp Trapp chair is the perfect example of how the detection of a need can initiate a product development process. In 1972, my eldest son was two years old and had outgrown his highchair. But we were unable to find any other chair that allowed him to continue to sit in a natural way and at a comfortable height at the grown-ups' table. My first reaction was that this was a pity, but as a designer, this discovery also entailed a challenge. The solution was to develop a chair of my own design that would be suitable for children of all ages.

The consideration that has had the largest impact on my design of sitting solutions is the fact that people spend more and more of their time sitting. The degree of physical passivity that characterizes modern life calls for improved sitting devices.

The act of observing

People who want to help shape human beings' material surroundings must be good at observing people's behaviour, at watching what people are doing. This is particularly true for people who choose to express themselves through functionality and problem solving. Observation in this context can be defined as the art of noticing one's own and other people's use of and interaction with the objects that surround us. We must ask questions about the usefulness of the tools and solutions that are already in use. The content in the previous section entitled "Favourite Postures", for example, is based on my own observations. The ability to observe in this way is rooted in an attitude or a special way of relating to the world. It is possible, in addition, to use some formal working methods during the observation process. Regardless of the actual technique used, however, the designer must have a consciously observant attitude.

When working with chair design, it is especially important to observe environments where people dare to heed the signals their bodies send them. To do so is to ascertain whether these people's use of their bodies differs from other environments where social codes force the body into prescribed, adopted postures.

Examples of useful observations
From your position in the queue at the bank, you can observe the bank clerks' working postures.

By simply strolling through an office, you can count how many people sit with their legs tucked under the chair and how many have their legs stretched out.

If we take a moment to study people sitting at a table, we might notice that their favourite postures are leaning far back or leaning forwards and resting their forearms on the table. There are very few people who sit at the angles offered by the designers of the traditional chair.

The same also applies when observing people sitting on a sofa or non-adjustable armchair. After sitting for a while, most people choose a more reclined posture for their upper body than the back of the sofa or chair is designed for. This means that their back is only supported at shoulder height, resulting in what I call a banana back.

If you observe customers in a furniture shop, you will notice how the visual form, rather than the function of a product, seems to be the deciding factor when people are looking for a piece of sitting furniture for their home. In some cases, people do not even try sitting on a chair before buying it.

It was this observation that made me come up with the following suggestion. Whenever two persons want to choose a piece of furniture, one of them should be blindfolded on the way through the shop and should remain blindfolded as he/she tries out the furniture on the showroom floor; then, on their way out, the other person should be blindfolded while trying out the furniture. This way both will have both seen and tried out the furniture separately.

Observing the discrepancy between the way chairs are normally constructed and the way they are used is the start of the creative process for finding better solutions

Mentally in the chair

When I first start working on a chair or another device intended for long-term sitting, I place myself on it, as well as in it, mentally – as opposed to merely visualizing it from the outside. When you sit on a chair, you don't see much of it, but you feel and sense it all the more. Later on in the development process, the aesthetic (visual) form becomes important, and this necessitates visualizing the object from the outside. The reverse procedure is true for chairs where the expression or the visual form is more important than the function.

Obviously, to begin by sensing the object as opposed to seeing it can result in entirely different forms than those that are generally accepted. Many of my chairs are meant to function as an extension of the dynamic human body. Frequently, this yields an entirely different form or expression than sitting devices that are initially sketched out in order to blend in with an architectural environment.

Dream design

One of the most common limitations in product development is conventional wisdom. It is precisely the desire to give free rein to innovative thought and free ideas that has caused the widespread use of work forms such as brainstorming and value analysis.

As a rule, the point in organizing such processes is to encourage the creative power of thought that we so frequently restrain in our effort to be as rational and socially acceptable as possible.

When we dream, these kinds of constraints remain dormant. This allows thoughts, ideas and experiences to intermingle without being constrained by conventions and inhibitions. The result can be enormous creativity as well as imaginative and unexpected associations between stored experiences.

When I wake up in the early hours of the morning, I often experience creative forces that are released in dreamlike fantasy. I lie half awake and think through the problems that need to be solved during the day ahead. I may go to sleep again and let my dreams grapple with this reality, allowing them to handle issues using their fabulous ability to solve problems. I can find the answer, when I am lucky, in an association between real, physical challenges and the unconventional chaos that is brought into play by dreams.

Is it possible that it is a capital error of priorities to want to cram as much measurable factual knowledge as possible into the minds of our schoolchildren? Do perhaps completely different stimuli exist for advancing humankind? Development of those parts of the brain that govern aesthetic and creative thought also entails developing our ethical principles. Alongside the deeper insight and pleasure derived from creating within the various creative forms of expression, this will also, according to brain researchers, increase our ability to make good decisions both for ourselves and for our planet.

The importance of leaving our descendants adequate resources and a viable environment is of increasing concern to me, and I think it is appropriate to make a few general comments concerning furniture in an environmental perspective, even though the topic lies somewhat outside the subject of this book.

I cannot claim to have had environmental awareness in all I have done as a designer, but there are two goals in particular that I have always pursued:
– To develop qualities in products that will hopefully result in a long service life
– To use natural wood, a renewable resource, to the greatest extent possible.

I have previously voiced a somewhat contradictory view of material products in general. In a world already overflowing with products, additional pieces of furniture add to the global problem of over-consumption. Hence it is important to be perfectly aware of their insignificance for our existence and standard of living. In the future we must all be more critical of the vast consumption of resources that furniture production represents.

It is fairly safe to predict that this aspect will play a far greater role in industrial design generally, and in the design of furniture in particular, than has been the case up until the present time.

Butterfly, 1996

Concept/design: Harald Røstvik/Peter Opsvik. A sculpture on wheels that aims to turn the spotlight on the sun and wind as sources of energy for the transport sector.

A global matter
– our responsibility

Anti-furnishing

As creators of goods for the modern market, whether as designers, manufacturers or suppliers, we cannot shirk our responsibility regarding the environmental issues that threaten the future of our planet.

At a minimum, we should apply basic eco-design tools such as guidelines and checklists. One useful approach is to analyse the input of resources and the environmental impact in the different phases of a product's life, integrating the context of the product and potential for new concept development. This checklist is used in UNEP's eco design handbook.

What we call furniture today was an unknown phenomenon in our distant past as nomads. We only started using tools to maintain and assist our bodies during the most recent eras of mankind's history, and even then, this was common only among a small, limited part of the population in the economically richest parts of the world.

One example of an ecological way of furnishing a home is the traditional Japanese way, whereby rooms are furnished with nothing more than a tatami mat. This could almost be called anti-furnishing.

If the tatami mat is an ideal for ecological furnishing (or lack of furnishing), perhaps our local, western cultures ought to learn from the principle and begin to keep furnishings to a minimum. We have grown accustomed to surrounding ourselves with an abundance of objects that we barely need. By concentrating on having fewer, better-quality possessions that can serve multiple purposes, we could probably attain greater personal happiness and at the same time save the environment from an unnecessary burden.

How can we imagine an "anti-furnished" office premises looking in the future?
When I practise the saxophone, I tend to walk around the room instead of sitting down. I find that I can practise for two to three hours straight, strolling around, without feeling the slightest bit tired. If I draw on this experience when trying to imagine a minimally equipped office, the result can be furnishing consisting merely of a few simple sitting devices scattered around the premises. Instead of being placed on a desk, the computer – in the form of a laptop – hangs in front of you like a saxophone, in a good working position, with attached earphones/microphone. You can walk around freely, stand in a dynamic way, or sit. When you wander around, you can either seek isolation or have contact with your colleagues, as you wish. In this way, a meeting between two people can consist of a stroll, with both bringing along their archives and communications facilities. If you want a bigger picture than the screen allows, you can get the laptop to project the picture onto a nearby wall.

If the work is carried out in a sitting position, the screen and keyboard will always be placed at a natural distance and angle, whether you are reclining or sitting upright. Tables can become quite unnecessary.

Fashion and the carousel of consumption

In the furniture industry, the long-lasting lines are called styles, while the shorter fluctuations are called fashions or trends.

Why do we have such rapid changes in fashion? For the end user, one positive thing about fashions in general, and furniture fashion in particular, may be quite simply that it is pleasant to have a change every now and again. But is this a tenable argument for the frequent about-turns in fashion? No, there is such a wide range of different products on the furniture market nowadays that it is fairly certain you would never have to buy exactly the same item again when you are looking to replace a piece of furniture. This would hold true even if there hadn't been any changes in fashion since you last went furniture shopping

It is deplorable that the rate at which items are replaced should accelerate simply because people feel miserable if they have last year's model – a model which they were perfectly happy with last year because it was generally declared at the time to be at the height of fashion.

Manufacturers may consider fashions profitable, as they are able to charge a higher price if they are at the forefront of the latest fashion. But when throngs of imitators appear on the scene with similar products, the price war becomes so intense that the pioneer is forced to change his products in order to keep profits up, hoping that he hits the nail on the head with the next new fashion.

These may be the basic mechanisms behind the rapid changes in fashion. New products appear in the marketplace without offering any improvement over the old one, other than being new. This type of product development leads to higher consumption and does not benefit the users or society.

When a designer is suggesting or deciding the visual form for a product, the above factors show that the task may be complicated. If form follows the short-term fashion trends, one may risk that the product will soon go out of fashion and will have an unnecessarily short lifespan. If the product has an appearance that differs radically from what's acceptable in its time, the risk is that the product will not gain widespread acceptance.

The solution for me has been that products with an unconventional functional solution have naturally enough also ended up with a distinctive visual form. Such products may experience longevity without being labelled as unmodern because they avoid following the patterns of short-term trends and fashions. I am bold enough to use my own chair designs – the *Tripp Trapp,* the *HÅG Capsico* and the *Håg balans® Vital* – as examples that prove advanced age is not necessarily synonymous with outdated appearance. All three chairs have been awarded the Norwegian "Classic Prize".

Heirlooms

I often wonder which products from our age will be handed down as family heirlooms to the coming generations?

In farming communities, buildings, furniture and tools are still passed on to the next generation when they take over the farm. Homes also tend to be left to the next generation, but the extreme mobility of the contemporary population means that it is less common today for children to move into their parents' or grandparents' vacated home than it was in earlier times.

Tools and instruments may be regarded as a part of an inheritance, but it is hardly likely that today's mobile phones, radios, food mixers, TVs, electric drills, cars and PCs will be highly sought after by our descendants. If they are kept at all, it will probably be as an oddity or antique.

Are cars handed down as heirlooms? Perhaps they are, to a certain extent, as curiosities or souvenirs.

What types of objects are not too large, do not become outdated, do not deteriorate, do not become unnecessary, etc.? One answer is products from industrial applied art such as glass, porcelain, cutlery (silver and steel) – and furniture.

Because this group of products distinguishes itself as especially suited for reuse, designers and manufacturers of furniture ought to feel a special sense of responsibility for ensuring that their products actually do have qualities that future generations might value, thereby giving these products a long service life.

This is also the reason why I recommend to people who intend to buy furniture to look for these qualities. You can make rapid progress by simply asking the following questions before making a decision: Will our descendants fight amongst themselves to own this, or will they argue over who is going to have to get rid of it? Will the Salvation Army be pleased to receive this item?

Surface treatment for lasting beauty

An important criterion for the longevity of a piece of furniture is that its beauty increases with use and age. From the standpoint of the conventional idea of durability and life expectancy of utility articles, it may at first sound impossible for wear and tear to enhance the quality of an object. However, this is entirely possible for furniture made of wood. It is paradoxical that we are so fond of old, rustic furniture, beautified by age and wear, that we are willing to pay large sums of money for such antiques, whereas at the same time most of us choose plastic-coated wood when we buy a new item. Lacquered wood is simply wood with a plastic coating. Lacquered wood might be considered beautiful in the "synthetic" sense of the word, i.e. without blemishes and pristine in appearance. The problem is that once the lacquer is damaged, as a result of an accident or wear or tear, the visual appearance can hardly be said to be beautiful any longer. A worn, lacquered tabletop has dirty edges and corners where the lacquer has worn off, and scratches and chips are extremely visible in any shiny lacquered surface.

By contrast, wood that has been left untreated or that has been treated with soap, lye, oil or wax will, if properly cared for, age and mature to have more and more character and will become more and more beautiful.

Replace or keep?

Which furniture will be kept for a long time and which will be thrown out after only a short period of time? The following list suggests some common reasons for keeping a piece of furniture:

1. Functions well
2. Easy maintenance
3. Replaceable parts
4. Timeless visual form
5. Appearance enhanced with age, or easy to renew
6. Easy to move and store
7. Strong product–user relation
8. Consciously selected by the owner
9. Uniqueness, originality or other sentimental values

The weakest link in a chair is often the fabric. If this is easy to replace, the chair's longevity will be increased considerably.

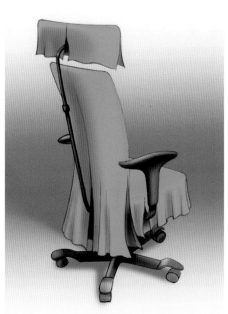

1992

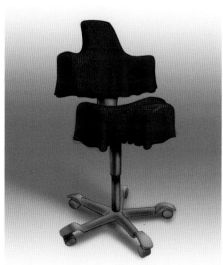

Paradox

Finally I would like to underscore a paradox in my profession, from an ethical point of view. I argue for a free and varied use of the (human) body, but end up designing products that add to the spread of the sedentary lifestyle. In a sense, these products can be seen as a kind of material painkiller for a general lifestyle disease.

When the planet is already overflowing with products, it may seem paradoxical to have a vocation that consists of developing new products. I am often in doubt about whether practising my vocation is beneficial or detrimental to society from an environmental perspective.

If serious industrial designers stopped practising their profession, what consequences would this have for product quality and consumption patterns? Would it lead to less consumption, or would the lack of design knowledge lead to an even greater abundance of horrible products? There is certainly no easy answer to this question, but it is my hope that products developed through devotion, far-sightedness and forethought will be less damaging to the environment and enjoy a longer service lifetime than products primarily developed in response to fashions and trends. The fact that furniture made by designers in the 1950s and 1960s is in demand on the used market today is an example of this.

I also hope that our profession can be called upon more frequently to solve problems facing the people who have the poorest living conditions on the planet. I am happy to have been involved in the founding and work of the organization "Design without borders" in cooperation with Norsk Form, the Norwegian Centre for Design and Architecture. This programme aims to utilize the creative and analytical skills of designers to help promote the development of new solutions in developing countries and areas struck by disaster.

Photographers:

Fredrik Arff: pages 89, 90, 194.

Asker foto-service: pages 9 right, 122, 125, 132, 137 top, 141, 171.

Studio Claerhout: frontpage, page 108.

Krister Engström: pages 107, 177.

Arne Hagen: pages 139 left, 157.

HÅG as: pages 9 left, 79 left, 80 left, 86 bottom
and top right, 87 right, 119 right, 129, 203.

Frode Larsen: page 109

Dag Lausund: pages 13, 24, 61, 62, 64, 66, 67, 68, 69,
96, 105 left, 119 left, 120, 134 bottom, 139 right, 161,
162, 163, 164 bottom, 165, 189, 191, 192, 203 left.

Lucretious/stockx: page 40.

Peter Opsvik: pages 17, 27, 47, 94, 102 top, 106, 113, 116,
121 bottom, 128, 134 top, 137 bottom, 138, 143, 148, 149,
150, 152, 153 left, 166, 172, 181, 196, 200, 202, 205.

Kolbjørn Ringstad: pages 114, 121 top, 159, 183.

Rybo: page 118.

Samfoto as: pages 29, 32, 34.

Stokke as: pages 76 left, 140 left, 160.

John Taylor/Alamy: page 6.

Odd Steinar Tøllefsen, pages 63, 65, 70, 71, 72, 73, 74, 75, 76 right,
79 right, 80 right, 81, 82, 83, 84, 85, 86 top left, 87 left, 91, 92, 93, 97,
98, 99, 102 bottom, 103,104, 105 right, 123, 124, 130, 131, 133, 135,
144, 145, 147, 164 top, 167, 173, 174, 175, 178, 179, 180, 182, 193.

Lise Aaserud/Scanpix: page 153.

Sketches:

Peter Opsvik: all sketches except:
Per Finne: page 205.
Per Olav Haugen, page 136, 137, 144.
Christopher Lightfoot: page 151.

Contact information

Cylindra as, Tusvik, 6222 Ikornnes, Norway
www.cylindra.no

HÅG as, pb 5055 Majorstuen, 0301 Oslo, Norway
www.hag.no

Naturellement as, Törla, 6020 Ålesund, Norway
www.naturellement.no

Peter Opsvik as, Pilestredet 27h, 0164 Oslo, Norway
www.opsvik.no

Stokke as, Håhjem, 6260 Skodje, Norway
www.stokke.com

Variér Furniture as, Håhjem, 6260 Skodje, Norway
www.varierfurniture.com

Note
*The manufacturers' Web sites contain updated lists of
dealers. The manufacturers' names are printed in capital
letters beneath the product photos in this book. If no
manufacturer's name is included, the product did not
have a manufacturer when this book was printed.*

Peter Opsvik's design team in 2007:
Tor Inge Garvik
Per Olav Haugen
Nils Seiersten
Anita Skogheim
Anders Ilsøy
Vidar Bråten
Geir Jarle Jensen